GOOD
DAUGHTERING

GOOD DAUGHTERING

The Work You've Always Done,
the Credit You've Never Gotten,
and How to Finally Feel Like Enough

ALLISON M. ALFORD, PhD

DEYST.

An Imprint of WILLIAM MORROW

DEYST.

FIRST EDITION

Designed by Renata De Oliveira

Library of Congress Cataloging-in-Publication Data has been applied for.

ISBN 978-0-06-343642-8

Printed in the United States of America

25 26 27 28 29 LBC 5 4 3 2 1

For my family, who truly sees

Contents

INTRODUCTION

When the phone rang and her mom's picture popped up, Maddie sighed and rolled her eyes. Then she told herself to get it together and answered the call. Ten minutes elapsed as Maddie listened to her mother vent about work, Maddie's dad, and even the shortage of treadmills at her mom's local community center. Maddie offered a few bits of advice but her mom didn't want to hear solutions; she just wanted Maddie to listen. And on most days, Maddie gave that to her mom and listened for as long as she could. Today, Maddie knew her mom had more to say, but she was impatient to get off the phone and get going with her own errands that were currently on hold for this phone call.

"I've gotta run, Mom," Maddie said.

"So soon?" Mom asked, and Maddie could hear the disappointment in her voice.

When Maddie was finally able to get off the call, she took a big, deep breath and audibly exhaled. She was late picking up her kids, ages 10 and 12, who needed her full attention after school, but she felt like her head was swimming with the noise of her mom's life.

It was true that Maddie felt deep pride in giving her mom emotional support. But she also felt worn out, and even a little bit guilty for cutting the call short. Maybe she hadn't said or done enough. Maddie knew she was expected to show up for her mom, no matter what, even if it meant shoving her needs to the side. That's just what daughters do, right? She sighed again and resolved to try harder next time.

Maddie's experience may be deeply familiar to you, if you're an adult daughter. The phone call, and the emotions it stirred up in her, may seem ordinary—and on the surface—there is nothing atypical about it. But conversations like this, with the accompanying energy and emotional outlay, are ways we show support to our parents, and they bind us together as family members. Daughters are often the glue holding everyone together. This is daughtering: it's the things women do for the good of their families.

Being a daughter can be a beautiful experience that is deeply rewarding. Whether you're a biological daughter or one formed through kinship, daughtering doesn't come without a cost. And doing daughtering is costing women a lot of valuable resources that are leveraged for the good of family and society. Daughters are the workhorses of family systems, the doers and the fixers, but along with this powerful role, there's also an all-too-common sentiment shared by many adult daughters: the belief that they're *not enough* or they're the *wrong kind of daughter*.

The truth is, Maddie is far from alone in her experience. And if I talked to her again today, I would tell her what my years of research demonstrate: that Maddie is doing a huge amount of daughtering—and that she is more than good enough.

In addition to a bachelor's degree in international studies from Texas A&M University, I have master's and doctoral degrees in the field of interpersonal communication from the University of Texas at Austin. I live and breathe the stuff of families, and in my research over the past decade, I have heard many women share these sentiments about their relationships with their parents again and again:

"She doesn't really know me."
"I love him so much, but it's hard to be his daughter."

"They just don't see me."

"I wish there was more to our relationship. But I'm not sure what else I can give."

"No matter what I try, I never feel like I'm quite doing enough."

So, I have sought, in my research, to answer the questions that plague so many women today: Am I living up to my parents' expectations of me as a daughter? Why does it seem easier for my sister than it is for me? How much more do I have to give to finally make my mother happy? How can I have a better relationship with my father without sacrificing too much of myself?

Over years of interviews and research, I have collected these and other common pain points for adult daughters and created research studies guided by what I have found to be the central questions that plague so many women: Why does it feel so difficult to be an adult daughter? How can women flourish in their families? How can we make the invisible work of families—most often done by women—visible and give it the recognition and praise it deserves? I have dedicated my professional life to uncovering these truths and puzzling out how to provide solutions for women who need it most.

Like Maddie, and like you, I am still working on how to be the best daughter I can be, balancing my personal needs with the demands of various relationships. I'm still figuring out where to draw the line between my needs and those of my parents, how to be good enough for them without abandoning myself.

I was raised by a mother and father who both experienced pain and trauma in their childhoods. Because of that, they worked tremendously hard to provide a different kind of life for me and my older sister, prioritizing honesty, clarity, and lots (*lots*) of conversation in our house. And that's what we had growing up: not a lot of money, but a lot of talking.

My mom became a licensed marriage and family therapist (LMFT) during my preteen years, and after that, she couldn't stop

talking about talking. She would describe what was happening between people on TV, or in real life, where it likely came from inside
of them, and what could be done differently. Growing up this way,
I began to see people and relationships like the script of a play, with
notes beside each character describing their emotional state.

Even with a lot of love in our home and people who were trying
very hard to be the best for each other, things still fell through the
cracks. Feelings got hurt. Sometimes we all felt unseen or unheard.
As a family, we were a bunch of good people who couldn't quite
give each other what we needed—at least not one hundred percent
of the time.

As I grew into an adult daughter, I began to notice the ways
I was consistently trying to be what my parents wanted me to be.
I sensed that the efforts I was making were necessary to keep our
relationship going, to be worthy of their admiration, and I worked
really hard to be good enough.

And that's why Maddie's story resonated with me. Many people
looking at her see a happy daughter and a great family, which are
true. She has smart kids and a considerate partner. She has parents
and in-laws who make an effort to stay connected and be respectful. So why did it all feel so overwhelming sometimes? Because
there's a lot that goes into making a flourishing family, or even just
a decent one. It's not magic; it's hard work.

Maddie was trying so hard to meet the needs of her preteens,
her mom, and so many other people who were counting on her.
And yet, even with good people around her who were loving and
trying their best, Maddie still felt tremendous pressure as she tried
to be the glue that held everyone together. She spent so much time
and energy thinking about what else she could or should do for
her parents and other family members. And a lot less time thinking about how great she was already doing or what she needed for
herself in order to feel good in the family.

While Maddie told me her story, I found myself thinking:
Why does she feel so much personal responsibility for creating
family connection? Why does she feel compelled to do so much,

even when she's burned out? And who is looking out for her emotional state? Why can't everybody see how hard she's trying and how much she's giving?

As a young adult thinking of my future career, I knew I could never be a therapist like my mom (I'm much too likely to say "suck it up, buttercup"). However, I felt deep down that I had to do something to help families, which led me to studying adult daughters and their mothers.

Over the previous decade, I have published groundbreaking articles on daughtering, starting a call-to-arms for fellow scholars to join me in elevating the role of women in families and making visible the critical role daughters play in nearly every community. While I didn't coin the term *daughtering*, I have done my very best to proliferate scholarship on the topic, emphasizing the importance of viewing the full complexity of women's experiences and emotions as important and meaningful. With colleagues, I published an academic textbook on mothers and daughters (*Constructing Motherhood and Daughterhood Across the Lifespan*). I created a podcast (*Hello Mother, Hello Daughter*) to connect my research with what people were experiencing in their lives. And after hearing from hundreds of women who shared the highs, lows, and mostly the in-betweens of being an adult daughter, I noticed something enormous: what they were *not* saying.

My research revealed the many ways women are hindered in talking about the role they play as a daughter: the invisibility, lack of language, the muddled understanding of the labor and resources needed for the role, and the guilt and obligation that is so often competing with a woman's personal well-being. It's no wonder we know so little about adult women doing daughtering; something has had a stranglehold over our expression of this critical role. And it is critical, for ourselves as individuals but especially for healthy families and a functioning society.

There is a large body of research showing how families are important to both the individual and society. However, the majority of our communication, psychology, and sociology studies prioritize looking at women with a maternal lens, meaning we think about women as mothers first. Daughters, in these studies, are the counterpart to the mother role. But I set out to do something different, and in my research, I cast the daughter as the main character. And I have sought to answer, what's important to women in the daughter role specifically? And how can knowing this information set us up to better support women, families, and a thriving culture?

Most of the stories in this book are about daughters and their mothers, as my research has also been. There's a lot of good science that demonstrates women are more connected to their mothers throughout their lives than they are to any other individual person. And the research shows that this relationship is particularly meaningful for both mother and daughter, even when the mother has died, and the daughter is left to carry on without her.

Only recently has my research—and the research more generally—turned more to an exploration of daughters and their fathers. Some of the manuscripts that are the result of this research are still in stages of peer-review, a process in academic publishing critical to ensuring only vetted, robust research reaches the final audience. Yet, through these investigations, I can say enough about adult daughters and their fathers that I am comfortable sharing with you some of the stories I have gathered along the way.

Some stories about fathers are told from the perspective of daughters who saw their fathers as a "separate entity" from their moms, due to divorce, widowhood, or similar circumstance. But mostly, I have noticed that daughters, when they mention their father at all, tend to lump him together with their mother, thinking of their parents as a unit, as in "they support me" or "they want me to visit." While fathers are critical to child development and families overall, the research shows less close communication, intimacy, and conflict for daughters and their fathers in adulthood. Many women (though not all) put dads on the "backburner" in family stories.

While the stories in this book include references to fathers, in-laws, stepparents, grandparents who are like our parents, "work dads," as well as the lady next door who is the mama of the neighborhood, mostly you'll read about daughters and their mothers. That's because when you ask women about being a daughter, they bring up the relationship with their mothers. Mothers and daughters are connected in a special way that creates great love—and sometimes great despair—for the women involved.

Given my area of expertise, everybody eventually asks me: What about me and my mom now? Did I write this book because I'm an expert in being the perfect daughter? Definitely not. Does my mother know me well? Yes, and in some ways much better than anyone else in the world. And also, sometimes there is a chasm of life experiences between us that can feel almost too wide to bridge. Between me and my mom, things can get complicated. There's a lot of affection and compassion and probably equal amounts of frustration and confusion.

But what's absolutely true is that I love my mom more than words can express. And that's something I have heard from many women over the past decade. That love, however, doesn't prevent the rest of the relationship from being, well, complicated.

And this brings me to the most common complaint I hear from adult daughters: No matter what women do, it never feels like enough. This is because the work women put into their families remains largely invisible—to society, to their families, and even to themselves. That is, adult daughters are *doing daughtering* to keep their families connected, and avoid pain and drama where they can, but they're not getting enough (or any?) credit for that work. Doing, in this sense, refers to the ongoing and active process of maintaining family bonds. Doing daughtering is seen through actions and relationship building. And daughtering is *definitely* work. Society ignoring that work is downright criminal if you ask me.

The biggest danger of ignoring this unpaid labor is that as women, we can lose sight of ourselves and agree with the world that we're not trying hard, we're not worthy, not a good enough daughter. And yet we can't stop ourselves from wanting to have that "good-enough" feeling. And this search for "enoughness" leads to sacrificing our time and energy for what our families (especially our mothers) need or want—or what we *think* they need and want. Our needs are being buried under a pile of other people's stuff.

Of course, there are daughters everywhere along the spectrum in their relationships with their parents, ranging from the terrible to the extraordinary. And I have spoken to all kinds of women in my research over the years. I conduct research using qualitative methodologies, where the goal is to understand people's thoughts, feelings, and experiences in their own words. Different from quantitative methods, the qualitative approach reveals how people talk about their lives and allows me to notice what they're *not* saying. The things that don't get aired are hidden, invisible, unnoticed, or seem so minor they are not worth mentioning; but I believe there is meaning in even the smallest moments of women's lives.

Throughout this book, I will share my research, asking women about doing daughtering, along with real-life stories of individual women. You should know that the names of the individuals and details from their lives have been changed to shield their identities, but the kernels of truth in their stories are real.

This book is specifically for women who are imperfect and who have real relationships with their parents that they might describe as the "messy middle." And what do I mean by the messy middle? I mean your relationship is neither truly awful nor perfectly wonderful, but somewhere in between. You're not suffering from toxic extremes, but you see that things between you and your parent could be better.

Daughters in the messy middle are in relationship with parents who they love, who do not suffer from personality disorders or experience abuse, but who remain imperfect, as are the daughters themselves. Women in the messy middle are balancing the interplay of multiple relationships—with their kids and partner and others—as well as work obligations, and social responsibilities that get in the way of having time to be the best daughter they might want to be. And their parents are experiencing the same pressures of spouse, community, siblings, career, and more, creating a dynamic that both forces them apart and draws them back together with their daughter. Daughters in the messy middle are looking around at each other, too, learning through participation in a daughterhood experience of women doing it together.

To best understand this messy middle, we need a new paradigm, one that is focused on how to help imperfect people—like most of us—with many demands on their resources to explore how we can all live more fulfilling, flourishing lives, even in the midst of all this mess.

As a communication scholar, I believe that an understanding of your identity and role in a relationship is central for understanding how we can better communicate. That starts by understanding how you think of yourself and others—a process that is always occurring inside of every daughter as she makes sense of the world and her responsibilities.

I also believe this piece of relationships—the identity of a daughter—is one that has been ignored for too long. Daughters deserve to understand themselves in their role and to make decisions based on that role. So you will find a lot of discussion of the self and processes for understanding your preferences as a daughter inside this book. But beyond the outward performance of daughtering that happens interacting with others, you deserve to understand the internal parts of daughtering. That means knowing what *you* need as a daughter from your own perspective.

My ultimate goal is to help you shift your entire mindset about daughtering. The activities in this book support that goal. At the end of each chapter, you'll find checklists, quizzes, writing prompts, and more designed to help you do the work of understanding and evolving your daughtering. The journey starts with recognizing what's already happening within your family, then moves into questioning and refining your role, and finally empowers you to make changes that feel meaningful and sustainable to you.

What you will find is that with a personal perspective shift, your family dynamics can change, too. Daughtering is an active role performance, and you can take action that makes a difference, no matter where you are on your journey. Whether you decide to do a little less daughtering and set some boundaries, or you find a way to engage in daughtering that feels more fulfilling, my hope is that after reading this book, you can approach daughtering in your family with more clarity and intention.

Above all, the goal of this book is to help you better enjoy your life and relationships. Women deserve to be happy, and we are agents of change in our own lives. Armed with the right knowledge and tools, you can make decisions for yourself as a woman in the world and inside your adult daughter role. You can improve your relationships, alleviate your most intractable personal conflicts, and find ways to flourish while doing daughtering.

In these pages, you'll learn to upgrade communication skills that can help you find a happier self and establish a foundation for a better family life. And the good news is that you don't need to overhaul your life to feel better in your adult daughter role. Small behavior changes and opening yourself up to a new way of thinking can reveal that there's so much you are already doing well. The key is to allow yourself to see daughtering as so much more than you've ever thought it to be.

Chapter 1
WHAT IS DAUGHTERING?

THE UNSEEN ROLE

What is daughtering? To answer that question, let's begin with a story. Jessa has two young kids and a husband. She's in the process of taking over the family business from her father, a third-generation restaurant owner, who is retiring. She's both incredibly proud but also feeling wary as she attempts to take on his legacy.

Every day she goes to work and tries to live up to the family name, meeting with suppliers and customers who ask about where her father is and when he's coming back. She sees a lot of emotions cross their faces when they discover that he's retiring and she, Jessa, is now in charge. And while she's running the café as her career, she's also a key contributor to her family's collective functioning and puts a lot of effort into keeping everyone connected.

Both her mom and dad are constantly in Jessa's space; they walk in and out of her house and the office at the café with little regard as to whether Jessa might be busy. A casual observer might think this is an idyllic family. Who wouldn't want two loving parents and the family business teed up for them? And yes, there's a lot of beneficial stuff going on here. But for Jessa, each day she faces the duality of doing a lot of daughtering without being fully seen as an independent woman who has control over her own life. And all Jessa's ever wanted is to be known, seen, and understood by her parents. She longs for their approval but never feels safe enough to let them see her authentic self—and her story is one shared by so many women.

So, what is daughtering and why does it matter? Daughtering naturally starts in childhood as girls interact with their parents, siblings, and extended family. However, even though women grow up, leave their parents' home, create families of their own, and live independently, daughters remain integral to the fabric of extended, intergenerational family life. But why has daughtering been overlooked in both societal discourse and academic research?

When I began my research, I read everything I could get my hands on about women, no matter what field of study it came from. I realized that daughterhood includes a wide spectrum of "typical" daughtering. Or, better said, there are millions of people across the globe who are doing daughtering—and as many ways to do it. But it was observable to me that there are "pockets" of daughtering rituals and behavior that belong to different cultural groups, with millions of women doing daughtering similarly to one another. On a population level, there could be infinite ways to do daughtering, and yet, we can still see patterns around the world of how women portray this role. I could see a treasure trove of women's experiences begging to be understood and acknowledged.

I dug deeper into the library, scouring the databases for more literature on daughtering. To my dismay, there was very little. So little that it seemed even the word *daughtering* was new to most people I shared it with. And so, I got to work. If nobody else was researching daughtering, it had to be me. What emerged was nothing short of a revelation.

I began to ask questions to learn how women understand their roles and how the roles of women are constructed over a lifespan. I analyzed what they said, and what they left unsaid. I found that adult daughters are really showing up for their families. Daughtering is embodied in everyday, ritualized practices to the extent that it's invisible. It is so habituated, normalized, and expected, that doing what adult daughters are supposed to do is considered rote, natural, or even trivial. Daughtering, it turns out, receives little notice, even from the women who are doing it. And yet, it requires quite a bit of effort and action.

In my doctoral dissertation and in follow-up publications, I shared the stories of women and how they described daughtering, turning that into a practical definition for the word *daughtering*: Daughtering is an adult woman's agentic behaviors as part of her family role in relation to her parent(s). Agency is our ability to act independently, make decisions, and shape the course of our lives. Therefore, daughtering encompasses all the ways adult daughters perform their role in relation to their parents. Agentic daughtering means adult daughters have choice in how they behave within this role, and while that sounds pretty simple, the reality of doing daughtering includes a nearly innumerable set of behaviors and skills.

Daughtering includes things like talking to their parents on the phone, asking about their lives or interests, planning family events, giving gifts, sending texts, acting as a translator, or teaching (like with technology or new jargon). Daughtering can look like going to dinner together or giving away your time or providing access to your children. Daughtering might be avoiding arguments and listening to something daughters don't want to hear. And daughters say the hard things that no one else will say.

Daughtering involves pushing back, holding space, and refusing to let something go. Daughtering may be thinking about parents' future needs and setting aside money. Daughters may investigate on behalf of their parents by talking to others about and for them. Sometimes daughters fight on a parent's behalf.

Daughters protect parents' feelings and prevent discord by avoiding topics or interactions that might cause pain. Daughters protect themselves similarly. Daughters repair and mend relational breaks, even those from generations back. Daughters can teach and incorporate new family trends. Daughters contribute to legacy-building. Daughters may share or distribute responsibilities among siblings, strategically, for the good of the family. And daughters can be daughters even when their parent is not nearby. The practice of daughtering is located in their heart and mind.

Can you picture yourself doing any of these things? Has it ever occurred to you before that these tasks created effortful and intentional (or unintentional) contributions to a family relationship? Pause for a moment and consider what that means to you now that you have this information.

Take, for example, the story of Analise. She is a friend of mine in her 40s, married with three kids (ages 12, 15, and 21), living parents, and several siblings (she's the eldest). She is aware that I study daughtering and we recently had a conversation about my research. As we were talking and I asked her about her role as a daughter, she said something along the lines of, "Well, I don't really do daughtering. Not like the way that you talk about it."

I thought she was kidding, but she wasn't. Analise is like so many women who tell me they are "not the right kind of daughter" for my research. They are sure that I'm looking to speak with someone who has it all together and finds no faults with her parents.

But that's just it, I'm not at all interested in the perfect daughters (because there are none). I want to hear from the woman who is doing the best she can in daughtering. That's the type of daughter who can reveal the true nature of daughtering. With that knowledge, I can translate the information into practical insights that help women flourish in their relationships.

I told Analise that I doubted she wasn't doing daughtering and then started asking some key questions about her relationship with her mother and father. By the end of our conversation, I was convinced she's a busy and productive adult daughter who is doing a lot to keep her family together.

Analise described multiple ways she was emotionally invested in her family, how she spent significant time attempting to please her mother and father, even taking on extra care of her paternal grandparents when her father could not. She also described how she was cognitively stuck, often thinking about the dynamics of her family life, and wondering what else she could do or how to make the system work better. This kind of comment is frequently shared when adult daughters describe their families. They get laser focused on doing more, anything that might solve the lingering problems.

Analise told me she hosts dinners for her extended family, including all the adult siblings, their kids, and her parents, who live nearby. But the most heartbreaking part of our conversation was when Analise told me that despite all of that "stuff" she was doing for the family, she feels like her parents "barely know her" and don't seem to know her children either (or wish to).

For her, the relationship was missing that intimate connection she considered to be crucial to successful daughtering. Without what she considered a "close bond," she was willing to dismiss all the rest of her planning and executing as simply "things women do in families because they're supposed to."

I asked Analise why she didn't talk to her mother about these feelings and wishes for a different relationship. Analise surprised me with her answer. She said that she didn't talk to her mother about this missing intimacy, because she didn't want to hurt her mother. Whoa. Analise was letting go of (or not pursuing) something she deeply wanted, in order to protect her mother from the emotional pain of this problem. Analise was constantly pulling from a deep well of daughtering, for the benefit of her family and her parents, while receiving shallow returns. And why? Why would Analise do this, over and over again throughout the years, when she is less-than-fulfilled? "Because," she said, "that's what daughters do."

This experience is happening for so many women, who are living and breathing their adult daughter role, but have no outlet to discuss it, no language for communicating their pain points, and an unclear way to quantify the costs of doing daughtering, leaving them feeling lost, alone, and confused.

WHAT IS THE WORK OF DAUGHTERING?

Daughtering is a multidimensional concept, which includes doing, feeling, thinking, and being labors. Fully understanding the labors of daughtering sheds light on the multiplicity of effort that it takes to keep a family together. Each of the four types of labor, discussed next, offers a unique perspective on how daughters contribute to, engage with, and shape their relationships and roles.

The Doing Work of Daughtering

Doing daughtering is the active way women show up to complete tasks and activities, using time and physical energy to attend to parents' needs. "Doing family" is not only a result of being in a family, but the very way that we create a sense of family. In your family, this could mean going to lunch with your dad or setting up a new app on your mom's phone. Doing daughtering means interacting with others and completing the activities that are assigned to your role—and since your work may not be obvious to everyone, doing family also includes telling others what you've done.

I call the task part of the adult daughter role *daughterwork*, a term adapted from the research on kin work and kinkeeping, which includes a large body of research going back decades on how families stay bonded. Kin work is a form of unpaid labor provided by relatives caring for one another with the goal of fostering meaningful connections.

Another example of daughterwork is using your time to check in on parents. One woman, Ella, told me she speaks to her father daily and her mother about four times a week, averaging about 150 minutes of weekly phone calls. That is time she could have spent on other tasks or chores but has allocated it to her parents. It's not just the work you do because you are supposed to—it's daughterwork.

The Feeling Work of Daughtering

The emotional labor of daughtering is vast and includes all the feelings of love and joy as well as the anxieties, worries, and guilt that women find in their family relationships. And while emotions are embodied and felt, the work of emotions speaks to control. Sociologist Arlie Hochschild described *emotion work* as the act of trying to change what one *is* feeling to what she believes she *should* be feeling in that moment. I call this the *daughtersentiment* part of daughtering; sensing, choosing, and enacting the emotions that come along with being an adult daughter, all of which requires giving of oneself.

Picture this: Your dad asks you to come to your grandma's house for a family gathering on Saturday. But you already had plans to hang out with friends. A feeling of annoyance washes over you, but you take a deep breath and try to change your attitude. Your family loves you and wants to see you. You pull yourself together and get in the right frame of mind, change your plans, and get ready to show up to Grandma's for the cookout. That's emotion work: when you give yourself a little pep talk and change your mind, heart, and attitude to align with what you think you *ought* to be feeling.

Unlike the daughterwork "doing" aspects of daughtering, the daughtersentiment "feeling" aspect is a process more than an outcome. And there is often nothing to show for completing some hardcore, strenuous, emotional labor. It happened inside your body. If there is a visible outcome, it might be at the cellular level where stress hormones can be measured. But unlike giving a tangible, wrapped birthday gift to your mom, the gift of daughtering emotion work is invisible. It is the gift of *not* arguing.

The Thinking Work of Daughtering

Mental, or cognitive, labor includes everything that a daughter gives mental space to, like thinking about organizing and managing everyday activities or planning for the future. Thinking work happens along the way to task completion (or the "doing" portion of daughtering), and I call this form of daughtering *daughterthink*. Thinking work includes strategizing or planning, monitoring, anticipating needs, and managerial oversight. Different from the doing of daughterwork, and the emotional weight of daughtersentiment, the intellectual aspects of daughterthink can take you both far into the past and well into the future as you assess how to perform your adult daughter role.

My friend Theresa told me a few years ago that she had started saving money for her parents in their later years. "I'm an only child. It falls on me. I have to prepare," she said. I asked if her parents knew that she was putting money aside and she said no. They didn't know and, if they did, they wouldn't like it. But Theresa is doing it anyway, both as a future gift to her parents and herself, who won't have to worry about having enough funds to cover their needs.

Just like a supervisor in a workplace might do, a daughter is aware of the many tasks and activities that need completing. She's thinking of all the moving parts but doesn't have her hand on each one. Research has shown that parents of young children often perform this type of supervisory care. They cook dinner in the kitchen while the kids play in another room. They're not staring at the kids directly, but they are monitoring with "one ear" on the sounds and activities. Researchers call this supervisory skill *metaparenting*. It seems reasonable to characterize a portion of the mental load of daughters as *metadaughtering*, which means an overall awareness and having "one ear" listening for any issues or concerns. It's not hands-on, but it's not completely hands-off either.

The Being Work of Daughtering

The last dimension of daughtering is identity formation. A woman's identity is who she sees herself as and the truths she believes about herself. Her identity goes with her into every role she plays, whether she is acting as a lawyer or class mom for the day. I call this dimension of daughtering the *daughterframe*. This aspect of daughtering is the least well understood when compared to daughterwork, daughtersentiment, and daughterthink, because your sense of self is so complex and multifaceted that it's not easy to encapsulate philosophical ideas into our everyday concept of what it means to be a daughter.

The daughterframe dimension of daughtering may be easiest to understand by imagining a specific context—a woman whose parent has died. Is she still a daughter? Does she still feel like a daughter? Think and act like her mother's daughter? Carry on the legacy of her father? Yes, she's a daughter for her entire life. Our identities are made up of traits and beliefs about ourselves that shape our worldview and outlook on life. As someone's daughter, you often represent yourself to the public using this identity.

Identity formation is both an individual act and a collective one, according to researchers. Doing the work of identity means figuring out "who I am" (just me), and "who we are" (collectively). At a social level, daughters recognize something in each other that connects us as a broader social group of women who share similar experiences and relational dynamics. In short, we belong to each other as adult daughters.

Take, for instance, the haircare line called "Carol's Daughter." The founder named the product after herself, using the position of her identity as someone's daughter to present herself to the world. Although Carol's name is on the bottle, we as the consumers are asked to see instead how founder Lisa Price views herself as moving through the world, especially in relation to beauty. And when the rest of us purchase this product because we are drawn to the name, we recognize the similarity of our own role as a daughter and validate the honor of fulfilling it as a group.

When asked how they represent their mothers in their daily lives even when their mothers are not around, women in my research have said things like "I have her laugh," and "I care about people like she does." Some have described doing the *opposite* of what they learned in their early family life. The aim of their daughtering is to change themselves, their children, and their destiny into something else because they learned what *not* to do as a daughter.

Through doing, feeling, thinking, and being, daughters enact their roles within families. Much of this labor takes time and effort, and yes, is hidden or invisible. We don't look at it or notice it, but we expect it to be there. Families thrive with adult daughters—and vice versa—who cultivate love, belonging, and legacy. In families with only sons, there are often daughters-in-law, nieces, and other female networks who fulfill this valuable role.

WHAT DOES DAUGHTERING LOOK
LIKE DAY-TO-DAY?

Daughtering happens in the powerful, but simple moments of your day-to-day life. While there are so many ways to do daughtering, later in this chapter, I'll describe the many things that do not count as daughtering. But first, I'll cover a few of the ways daughtering shows up in the ordinary moments of women's lives.

Daughtering Is Active and Agentic

When daughters do daughtering, they are not merely respondents to the parenting being offered but can act and react in such a way to produce the results they desire. When I spoke to women about their role as a daughter, they gave me examples of the ways they shaped their relationships, from the amount of calls they made to their mothers, to the amount of information they kept private to protect themselves or avoid conflict. Yet, many women I speak with are still unclear on what it means to *do daughtering*. They can describe the behaviors but not define the role.

This is the first important step on your journey to improving your life and family relationships: Define and recognize daughtering in your own life and in the lives of others. Only with this critical mindset shift can the work of embracing your role as a daughter begin; afterward, you can change it as much or little as you desire.

Daughtering Is Something We Embody—
but Not Something We Talk About

When we attempt to discuss daughtering, women often lean on borrowed vocabulary. They say things like "We're best friends" or "I'm mothering my mother now." What word do you use when trying to say so much about what is between a woman and another person she loves, a word that includes love, connection, responsibility, affection, obligation, as well as cultural weight? Without adequate vocabulary, any attempt to name and define something so subjective and ineffable will fail to capture the whole of it.

That's what happens when we borrow words to describe doing daughtering.

Take the phrase "best friends," which some women use to describe their mother-daughter relationship, and let's unpack what it really means. Consider your own close friend. What characterizes your relationship? You have a good time together, you laugh together, and you share common interests. And, what if she decided to stop being your best friend tomorrow? Would you be tied to her for the rest of your life? Decades of thinking about her every day? Or would you move on and find someone new to share your life with? Perhaps you've already had many friends who come and go in your life.

Friendship, by its very nature, includes the agency to maintain the relationship, and the choice when to let go and move on. Friendship is characterized by peer-like experiences, connecting with people around your age or life stage, matching you in career, education, children, health, income, marital status, and so on. You've got a lot in common with your friends.

Daughters and their parents do have lifelong histories and share identity traits that are linked to one another and their broader shared family. But daughters and their parents are likely to find any lasting separation and estrangement challenging; the other person will remain in their heart and mind for the rest of their lives. Instead of considering the points where "best friend" and "daughter" overlap, when we consider the differences most acutely, it quickly becomes apparent that parents in relationship are not quite the same as friends.

Take what Grier Shields said about her superfamous mother, the actor, model, and author Brooke Shields, in an interview: "I feel like we're now friends. You still discipline us, but I feel like we're much closer." Let's break this down. Do you have *friends* who discipline you? Unlikely. The presence of a disciplinarian indicates a power difference inherent to mother-daughter relationships.

Notice the words at the end of the quote. "Closer" is used to convey the current emotional bond. These words indicate a connection or bond between daughter and mother, regardless of hierarchy. Closeness is a social construct, meaning it's a way of thinking about a relationship and using language to describe it that others in our social system can understand. Closeness, as in this quote, signals a lack of conflict, an ability to communicate openly, and a release from the structures that create tension with parents, like financial dependence and curfew restrictions.

Let's talk about the use of the word "friend" to describe a mother-daughter relationship. Using the term "friend" or "best friend" to describe a relationship creates a bit of a problem. When daughters use the idea of friendship to describe a relationship for that different kind of role and bond between two people, it's confusing. This confusion can only be solved by using different language that better suits the relationship and more accurately describes what's going on between a daughter and her mother.

Likewise, if you hear someone talk about mothering their mother, another kind of confusion is created. Incorrectly labeling daughtering as mothering creates semantic overload, a linguistic concept that describes when a word carries too many meanings, interfering with our understanding of the speaker's intent. But this happens when daughters do not have alternatives to describe our lived experience that convey meaning with specificity. We end up using words that sort of convey our meaning, as best as we can articulate it.

But why do we not have the right words to talk about our daughter role if it's something we're doing all the time across our entire lifespan? One reason for this lack of daughtering vocabulary comes from society's tendency to prize women as maternal figures over other roles. You name what you care about in your social system, and ours cares about women as mothers. But when we frame women as mothers and use a maternal lens to discuss the fullness of women's lives, we cause two issues: (1) we create problems for mothers by piling the workload too high, and (2) we continue to devalue the necessary role of daughtering in families and in society.

Using specific and meaningful terminology to describe women's lives and their relationships brings a lot to the table. We add richness to the human experience when we call daughtering by its true name. When we notice and comment on women's unique contributions to families and society, we show that female labor, in its many forms, matters. Discussing our humanity and daughterhood with accurate language also aids others in noticing our efforts, providing a means for effectively discussing our lived experiences as daughters.

To summarize, using the word *daughtering* to describe all the ways you daughter over a lifetime with your parents helps women in several ways. Our language reflects our culture and what we care about, so updating your vocabulary is a move in the direction of valuing women in their daughtering role.

Daughtering Is Happening in Everyday, Routine Moments

When women detail their daughtering behaviors, they often cite things that are mundane, unremarkable, and even tedious, whether it's sending a voice note, adding events to a shared calendar, or thinking about a future trip. So, what makes these daughtering behaviors intentional? They were reported as being done *for the purpose of* connecting with family members or contributing to a thriving relationship. These were behaviors done for others or the greater good (with some benefits to the daughters themselves, of course).

Daughtering, it turns out, is not very flashy. It's simply consistently showing up for the good of the relationship. But the experience of being a daughter is an embodied one. You live inside the role and absorb how to do daughtering from social and cultural experiences. Since birth, you have been someone's daughter. At least, biologically, though perhaps not emotionally, you've been connected to a parent your whole life. And every day of your life, you have practiced that role and come to know it well, including the nuances and tensions associated with it.

Over many days, months, and years, you have embodied—or filled out—the role of a daughter. Embodiment acknowledges the body as the conduit for experiencing and interpreting the world around you. And in that body, you enact routine practices that can often be taken for granted or feel obligatory. Women doing daughtering are living out their role as a function of habit, as a practiced behavior that they simply *know* how to do, perhaps are even expected to do—because women's bodies are the site of social expectations, many of which are passed down to us from our parents.

Daughtering Is Resource Dependent

A resource is anything that a person values. There are object resources, which we can use in daily life, like a reliable car for visiting family members or a working cell phone with the bill paid. Another kind of resource is a condition resource, which are valuable in and of themselves, like good health and well-being, a peaceful state of mind, or a happy marriage. Next, there are personal characteristics resources, which are the traits or skills you have that help you manage stress or gain additional resources, such as self-esteem, good communication skills, or resilience when navigating chaotic family dynamics. There are also energy resources, which are valuable because they can be exchanged for other resources, including time, money to support your family, knowledge, or mental space for creative brainstorming.

Daughtering is an activity that can either fill or drain a woman's reserve tank. You have a limited amount of resources, which must be spread across all areas of your life. That's why it's important to carefully assess how and when to expend a resource on doing daughtering. You have to be sure you have enough to spread around for all your roles, or you will run out and potentially burn out.

Your resources can be filled up again, though, with behaviors like social support, affection, and self-care. Whether it's getting a hug from a friend, listening to a podcast that validates your experience, or crying to release any guilt, many things can help fill your resources back up to the top. Being part of a family is often a comfort and an asset to many women. For example, Brandi, a twenty-something daughter, shared with me that every day she speaks to her dad on the phone during her drive to work. It's a ritual of daughtering that benefits both of them, but especially supplements Brandi's reserve of confidence, happiness, and identity as she prepares to tackle her workday.

Daughtering Is Framed by Context

Daughtering is a socially situated endeavor, which means we can only understand the roles and responsibilities of women within the context where it occurs. Daughtering may look quite different from one family to the next, one generation to the next, or for those of varying socioeconomic means. Perhaps you call your mom every week on Sunday and go on an annual cruise with her. Your friend, on the other hand, never calls her mom, but she does send her money every month and a plane ticket to come visit her each summer. There are as many ways to do daughtering as there are parenting styles or romantic relationship exchanges.

Women around the world are expected to daughter differently based on religion, culture, and even geography. These expectations are shaped by gender, generational differences, customs, or even by who leads your country. These different contexts, in turn, shape a daughter's relationship with her parent.

I was talking with my friend, Yumei, who is from Taiwan, and she was telling me about her relationship with her mother and how they have come to an understanding about Yumei's sexuality. "She pretends it doesn't exist," she said. Yumei does tell her mother about the people in her life (friends and partners alike), her activism, and even her career path that includes running for local office. And when Yumei talks, her mom seems to listen. She doesn't leave the room or hang up the phone, but neither does she ask questions nor comment. It's an unsteady peace that is functional right now. And what about her dad? He has a different set of expectations, and the relationship remains on uneven ground.

In her family, Yumei is confronting the lifelong expectations her parents have had for her daughtering as an adult, and, politically, she's helping to manage her parents' fear of her vulnerability as a key figure for LGBTQIA+ rights in a time when political relations between Taiwan and neighboring countries remain tense. Yumei's story is uniquely her own, but there are nuggets of authenticity that resonate with all daughters of different cultures and contexts.

While your daughtering may be influenced by other social factors, it continues to exist within a system that influences your behaviors and expectations.

WHAT DAUGHTERING IS NOT

When I tell people that I study daughters, almost everyone comes up with a story of a female child in their lives. "No," I respond, "I mean adult daughters, like you and me." This reaction underscores exactly why clarifying what daughtering is—and especially what it is not—is essential. Daughtering is not confined to your early years. It is not defined solely by obedience or caregiving. It's not fixed or static, nor is it limited to a single set of prescribed behaviors that you must follow throughout your life. Daughtering is far richer and more complex than any of that; it evolves with your life circumstances, and is shaped by your family history, cultural expectations, and personal experiences.

Daughtering Is Not the Same as Caregiving

Sure, daughters can and do provide care to others, especially parents. In fact, there's a large body of research showing how adult children care for aging and ill parents. That research, interestingly, finds that daughters are the most likely care providers for aging parents, but only if they are living geographically closest. If not, the care provisions shift either to a son or a daughter-in-law. The key takeaway, however, is that this is not what *all* daughters do. The role portrayal begins much earlier in life and encompasses much more within it.

Imagine you were a member of a sorority in college. Long after you left school and even when none of your sisters are in your area, you still have a sense of belonging in this group and playing the part of the membership can be true at all times, 24/7, 365 days a year. Similarly, take a yoga instructor. They can do yoga for pleasure, to make money, or to foster their identity as someone who sees the world in a certain way. Being a yogi is a worldview and a collection of essential skills. And the same is true for adult daughters. Your role lasts a lifetime, and the portion of adult daughtering is enacted over decades. It would be ungenerous to relegate the role of daughter to only what you do when your parent is older.

Daughtering Is Not Only the Transition Through Adolescence

Recalling the shift from child to teen is easy for most of us, and we can pinpoint many daughtering events that occurred. For many women, the time in your life where you begin to find your own identity, in adolescence and through young adulthood, is deeply meaningful. It's natural that this stage might come to mind, because it is a turning point for many women in how they began to communicate with parents, transitioning from the ways of childhood ways into something different.

We tend to notice and remember events, conversations, and interactions around turning points in our lives because the big moments in life are important and we can easily recall them.

But those big moments are just one part of what it means to be a daughter. And adolescence is marked by a very different set of rules between daughters and their parents than what you experience as a financially and legally independent adult. The key takeaway here is that the experiences of teen years are *part* of your daughtering experience, but they are limited to a short time span in your life, whereas daughtering continues for the rest of your days.

Daughtering Is Not Only for Biological Children

Many daughters are adopted and raised by nonbiological parents. Some daughters have multiple mothers in the form of stepmothers or grandmothers who mother for a time when their moms cannot. Or maybe you have both a bio and nonbio mom.

A limited body of research explores how women reframe themselves and their parents after a long separation, whether it's from adoption or living transnationally. Key findings from these studies show that women can hold on to the idea of multiple mothers, both those proximate and distant or even unseen. Then, when daughter and mother reunite, the daughter participates in active negotiation of reintegrating this added mother into her life. The agency and decision-making that women demonstrate in these times, whether welcoming, reluctantly accepting, or gatekeeping, is part of doing daughtering for women with multiple parental figures.

These studies have shown how women allow both biological and nonbiological mothers to be important to them, demonstrating that part of daughtering is deciding how, when, and in what ways to receive mothering (and fathering).

Women gain and lose mothers and fathers in our lives through myriad ways. In marriage or legal partnership, you can gain in-laws and a whole new set of expectations for doing family and daughtering. Whether you mold yourself to these new expectations (or adjust your family members to yours) being a daughter to a parent is as simple as allowing yourself to embody the role. You might even lay claim to daughtering your neighbor who lives alone, providing a listening ear or watching golf together.

Daughtering Is Not Only for Those Whose Parents Are Alive

Every year on Mother's Day, I go online to see a slew of messages from daughters and sons to their parents who have passed away. If you were to think of daughtering as only the daughterwork part, where you complete tasks for, interact with, and visit your parent, then you might miss this important feature of the role. A daughter is a daughter for her whole life. Whether your parent is across the room, on the other side of the globe, or has died, you can be doing daughtering. You are born a daughter and you die as one. And that's not something every woman can say about all the social roles available to us.

There are more things that are not *daughtering than can be covered in* this text, but this list is a good one to keep the parameters clear. Allowing yourself to think of daughtering in new ways opens up a vast landscape of possibility. In parallel, we can think of anything a woman does as feminine. If you think of anything a daughter does as *doing daughtering*, it becomes less constrained by what you thought you knew it to be and opens you to a new interpretation.

Daughtering Includes Eliciting Parenting

While many features of daughtering require giving, it's important to note that daughtering can also mean receiving. Lottie, 31, described how recently, when she was sick, she got worried and called her mom on the phone at 3 a.m. to ask her what she should do. Her mom answered her, soothed her, and told Lottie she should probably go to the hospital. Lottie told me that it was a little embarrassing to share that story, as she's probably too old for that kind of thing and already has a family of her own. But then she went on to say that she didn't know what to do and so she called her mom, and she's glad she has the type of mom who will pick up her phone in the middle of the night.

When I think of daughters seeking out the mothering or fathering they need, I light up. I adore this facet of daughtering that acknowledges women's agency and power in any relationship. You are able to take care of yourself. And you may do it in any way you wish, even if it means calling your mom. Janneke van Mens-Verhulst described daughtering thusly:

> Women can be said to be daughtering because they are assumed not only to receive care and authority, but also to elicit it when they are in an originally dependent relationship that involves being looked after by more powerful people; people who are perhaps older, wiser, or more qualified. The concept emphasizes that daughters actively organize their safety and freedom but does not define how they do it. Daughters may wallow in the love, welcome it, resist it, or try to reciprocate; they may accept the authority, avoid it, withstand it, or try to negotiate.

Wallow. Welcome. Accept. Negotiate. These active verbs describe how daughters elicit the daughtering they desire. Daughters know how to draw out the parenting they need. Resist. Avoid. Withstand. Daughters can put up barriers when necessary.

Meryl was one among many women who described needing and getting childcare help from a parent. While the childcare itself is grandparenting, it is the *requesting* of the help that features daughtering. Meryl, who is 29, described having a deep desire for equal attention from her mother as her siblings received, and for her mom to have mindful interactions with her kids. For Meryl, having her mom's attention on her kids was more than simple childcare—it was a validation that her life was important. She said, "In the long run, I just want my kids to have a mentor and somebody they could go to." Meryl went on to describe many negotiations around this topic, as her mom didn't quite understand the importance or value her time being spent in the same way.

The asking, negotiating, and even button-pushing that daughters do with their parents is a key feature of daughtering that can often be overlooked. But daughtering stems from a dyadic role portrayal, one that features a pair: daughter and mother or daughter and father. It is within this push-and-pull of two individuals that daughtering is enacted, framed, reframed, negotiated, and reified, becoming something new. It's a two-way street.

Daughtering Is Saying the Difficult Thing

Daughters say the hard things that no one else will say. You bring up the topics that your parents need to hear, even if they don't want to. Daughters aren't being pushy when they push back; it's being direct because you know it's what the relationship needs.

About a year ago, I was interviewed by a graduate student, Valentina, for her research project. I was immediately intrigued when Valentina opened our conversation by introducing herself as a *bully daughter*. She told me, "I push my mom around. I think I may have misused my position as the eldest daughter and turned my parents' lives upside down. My mom says that I am a bully of a daughter." She laughed, but I could hear some hesitancy in that laughter.

She was both proud and simultaneously a bit embarrassed to share her "bully daughter" moniker. On the one hand, it suited her personality and positioning within her family, including how she resisted her mother's mothering. Valentina called up the trending topic of the *eldest daughter*, very hot in US media, referencing a shared ideology of oldest daughters as workhorse parent-helpers who assist with (or take charge of) the running of the family; but she turned this paradigm on its head, saying that she acts as the alternative—a demanding daughter who takes more than she gives. But as Valentina described the nickname, she was also sharing that she knew this behavior to be renegade, making her another "wrong kind of daughter," an outcast among women who are *not* supposed to act that way.

Though she blacklisted herself as "not-the-right-kind-of-daughter," Valentina was self-identifying with a key feature of daughtering, which is saying what needs to be said, even when it causes tension or conflict. That takes courage and means staying true to yourself and what you believe. It's a form of being a daughter that diminishes harmony in families—but for a greater good that benefits the family.

In my family, I'm often the *bringer-upper* of difficult things. I ask my parents about all kinds of topics, many of which they prefer not to discuss, which is an important aspect of being a daughter: bringing change to a family that needs it. Sometimes it requires a lot of courage because I know it will make someone uncomfortable or even angry. But I decided that it's worth the risk if I accomplish something through my verbal poking and prodding.

Every daughter has a threshold for creating that same kind of discomfort and it's up to you to decide what's worth having people squirm about. Whether it's health or finances, or a guideline for being around the grandkids, bringing up the things that need to be said can push everyone into a better place as a family.

Daughtering Is Being a Parent's Delegate

Daughtering can mean acting as a proxy for your parent. Daughters often talk to others about their parents on their behalf. They seek out their best interests by going ahead of them and removing barriers. They fight their battles. Daughters make connections within communities and families.

When I spoke to Sabine, she told me that she's an intermediary between her mom and brother because Sabine worries that her adult brother is leaching their mom dry. He is unemployed, living at home, and plays video games all day. To top it off, he's also disrespectful to their mom. Sabine has taken it upon herself to "get after" both mom and brother about the situation, telling her mom how to set better boundaries while coaxing her brother to shape up. Sabine has the challenge of standing up *for* her mother *to* her mother.

Similarly, Jenny told me how she is known in the family for safeguarding her mom. Her niece now fears her, because several years ago Jenny lost her temper when the girl was disrespectful. "I walked in deep red and shaking, picked her up and took her outside and had a very stern—but not yelling—conversation with her about how she will never disrespect my mother again," Jenny relayed. Laughing, she adds, "Scared the bejeebers out of her." Jenny was proud of that moment, telling me her mom deserves respect, and she was going to be the one to make sure she got it.

Daughters Are Shields

The protective instincts of daughters can also extend to shielding parents from life's challenges. Daughtering can mean protecting parents' feelings and preventing discord by avoiding certain topics or interactions. One of my best-known quotes among my friends is "Daughtering means knowing when to keep your mouth shut." Daughtering can mean allowing parents to keep their secrets, or facilitating an easier life for one's parent, in whatever way works best for you and them.

Daughters Are Fixers

Daughtering often means being the family fixer. Daughters repair and mend relational breaks, even those from generations back. Take Janet, who at age 58 realized her family had spent decades silently avoiding conflicts rather than working through them. When Janet's mom and aunt had a falling-out years ago, the silence lasted. Their relationship had grown into one of bitterness and separation, the impact of which was trickling down through the cousins and grandchildren. Everybody was talking about it in the family's private Facebook group, regularly chatting about what to do, taking sides and rehashing old news. Janet decided that if anyone could do anything about this gaping wound, it had to be her. She organized a family reunion, and she coaxed both mom and aunt to attend. She didn't ambush them but let them know that it was time to have real, meaningful conversations. Janet spent hours on the phone, carefully listening to each person's story, mediating misunderstandings, and helping family members rediscover empathy.

Daughters break old patterns and make new ones. Janet's way might not work for every daughter, but it made an impact on her family. Her thoughtful intervention led to breakthroughs that got the wheels moving toward healing. It wasn't easy, and Janet's mom and aunt were frequently annoyed with her while the cousins told her it was no use. But through repeated, thoughtful efforts, Janet made progress. And she wasn't just fixing the immediate tensions—she was rewriting her family's relational script, laying healthier foundations for generations to come. That gave Janet satisfaction in her efforts.

Daughters Are Coaches

Daughters can teach new family trends, leading families into new ways of being and connecting with each other, while helping everyone adapt to the culture and context they're living in. Think about Lillie, a 27-year-old daughter who noticed that family gatherings always seemed to end up tense or awkward. To lighten the mood, Lillie started encouraging her family to share "highs and lows" at these dinners—a simple practice she learned from her friends when they would get together and tell each other their week's best and worst moments. At first, Lillie's parents were skeptical and resistant, as it was not typical in their family to share feelings or anything mushy that might make you vulnerable in front of others. But after a few tries, it started getting easier. They found a few moments where conversations flowed more naturally, they laughed at a few things, and many of the old, tense ways of talking were avoided. Lillie had coached them into a new way of doing family dinners.

GETTING RID OF THE WRONG
DAUGHTERING IDEAS

There are a lot of misconceptions and misunderstandings that persist around the idea of daughtering, and for good reason. It's hard to talk about and society hasn't been doing much talking on the topic. How can it be that even those doing daughtering can so easily mistake and misunderstand it? Or at the very least, why have we found ourselves unable to talk about a role that is so rich and gratifying, yet also so costly? The answers to these questions and more will be explored throughout the upcoming chapters. For now, you might be wondering what is the danger of misinterpreting something as benign as doing daughtering? The problem is that when we misrepresent daughtering, we miss an opportunity to see women in their full humanity and complexity across a lifelong role that is deeply embedded in our everyday lives. Psychologist Carl Jung said, "Until you make the unconscious conscious, it will direct your life and you will call it fate." The remedy, where daughtering is concerned, is to point out and call out the behaviors you see yourself and others doing, bringing these behaviors into social consciousness.

ACTIVITY 1: QUIZ FOR DAUGHTERING WORK

I challenge you to think about the many ways you do daughtering, particularly the less-obvious behaviors. Remember, daughtering can show up as doing, feeling, thinking, or being work. Allow yourself to respond to this quiz with an open mind and pay careful attention to your responses. When responding to the following prompts, think of yourself and one parent. For each line, score yourself from 1 to 5, based on how much you are doing this form of daughtering. One point means you do very little of this daughtering action, while a score of 5 means you do a lot.

QUIZ FOR DAUGHTERING WORK

Parent name: ....

	Daughtering Forms	Description	My Score, 1–5 points
	Daughterwork		
1	Practical Efforts	I support my parent with practical help. (Examples include helping with tech, errands, taxes, household tasks, and lots of other things you can add.)	
2	Planning and Hosting	I initiate and plan family gatherings, celebrations, or outings to keep us connected.	
3	Tradition and Legacy	I proactively maintain our family traditions and also start new ones.	
4	Decision Involvement	I stay involved in my parent's major life decisions like living situation, finances, or their future.	
	Daughtersentiment		
5	Providing Affection	I express love, gratitude, appreciation, or affection to my parent regularly.	
6	Emotional Availability	I offer emotional support and allow for hard conversations with my parent.	
7	Meaningful Presence	I'm present and engaged during our time together, prioritizing meaningful connection over the superficial.	
8	Supporting with Empathy	I listen, empathize, and comfort my parent when they're struggling.	
	Daughterthink		
9	Monitoring and Anticipating	I check on my parent's well-being and anticipate challenges or needs on their behalf.	
10	Calibrating and Flexibility	I assess and recalibrate my daughtering to match changing needs and life circumstances, both mine and theirs.	
11	Reflecting and Improving	I regularly reflect on my role as a daughter and consider how I can better show up in the relationship.	
12	Collaboration Efforts	I communicate and coordinate with siblings to support our parent together, sharing what I know and learning what they know.	
13	Fairness and Equity	I balance attention and support toward each of my parents, treating them fairly in comparison with each other.	
14	Boundary Setting	I set and communicate reasonable, healthy boundaries to protect my time and energy (and that of my partner and children).	

	Daughtering Forms	Description	My Score, 1–5 points
	Daughterframe		
15	Considering the Self	I view *being a daughter* as an ongoing part of who I am—not just something I do.	
16	Public Awareness	I talk about being a daughter with others, owning this identity publicly and personally.	
17	Relational Encouragement	I encourage and enable healthy relationships between my parent and our other family members.	
18	Culture and Religion	I support my parent's cultural and religious values. I also engage in these beliefs and foster them in my children, as far as they align with my own values. (Examples include celebrations, food, or dress.)	
19	Respectful Interactions	I show respect through my actions and attitude, even during disagreements.	
20	Navigating Conflict	I try to resolve conflict with maturity, avoiding toxic behaviors or escalating. I try to avoid letting things fester or become chronic.	

SCORE: ....

out of 100

NOTE: Add up all your points from the above rows. Record your score.

My score in relation to my mom (or dad/in-law/stepparent/other parent) is: ....

out of 100

SCORE CATEGORIES

20–55 points | Attentive Actor

You are actively contributing and doing a lot of daughtering for your parent. You've started to recognize the various ways you support your parent, both overtly and subtly, and in different forms. This growing awareness helps you see the extensive nature of your efforts, allowing you to conceptualize daughtering as significant work. You are becoming more attuned to how these efforts—which might have previously felt routine or invisible—contribute substantially to your parent's well-being and the complete family dynamic. Your score reflects the amount of daughtering you are currently giving, which you can decide to increase, decrease, or keep exactly the same.

56–75 points | Committed Carer

You are an engaged daughter, providing substantial support provisions. You might be surprised by the extent of your daughtering efforts, as you're likely doing more than you initially realized. This deeper recognition of your role highlights how your consistent involvement impacts both your parent's and your own life.

76–100 points | Aware Anchor

You demonstrate intense dedication to your daughtering role. The vast array of daughtering you undertake, encompassing both visible and invisible efforts, permeates your life. You are alert now to the extensive nature of your involvement, from daily tasks to emotional support and beyond. This awareness reflects how deeply your daughtering efforts integrate into your life, reinforcing the need for a balanced approach to daughtering while maintaining other responsibilities.

Next Steps:

Option 1: Take the quiz again, answering based on other parents in your life, like a stepparent or in-law. Does your score change when you account for daughtering a different parent? Do you notice that you are providing more or less daughtering labor to one parent over others? Or perhaps you are providing different types of daughtering to this parent or that one. Taking the time to evaluate where and how you expend your daughtering efforts can give you data to reflect on.

Option 2: Take the quiz again, answering on behalf of your sister (if you have one), selecting the same parent to consider. The goal for this activity is not to point out stark differences or unfairness in relationships, but rather to make visible the ways your sister is doing daughtering *differently* and yet still credibly. *Try* to respond to questions based on what you have observed between your sister and parent. But also look for ways your sister does daughtering that have not been very obvious to you before today. There may be some questions where you need to guess to provide a reasonable score, and that's okay. Again, the goal is to try to see the daughtering your sibling provides to make the invisible labor connecting families into something visible and valuable. Complete the quiz as many times as necessary to explore your relationship with different parents and siblings.

Sibling's score with (mom/dad/in-law/stepparent/other) ....
(based on your best guesses).

Although this quiz is about daughtering—the labor provided by a female adult child to her parents—it may still be useful to think about types of invisible labor that other members of your family do. For example, you might think about the kind of work your partner does for your mom or dad, or notice how a brother participates in important family bonding. While these labors have very different expectations than for women doing daughtering, you may find that some invisible efforts made visible to you help you begin to detect the hidden work present in other areas of your life.

Now it's time to evaluate what you learned from this activity. The goal of this quiz is only to help you *notice* daughtering in its many forms. What was surprising to you in this quiz? What do you notice about your scores? What areas of daughtering were made visible to you? Jot down a few notes here for you to consider:

DAUGHTERING INSIGHTS

_____

_____

_____

_____

_____

_____

_____

If it feels safe and comfortable, take some time to compare your own daughtering to others.

You can take the quiz repeatedly, considering different parents (mother, father, in-laws, stepparents) and your sisters, stepsisters, and sisters-in-law. This tool is _not_ meant to help you take a victory lap, pointing out the disparities to win some kind of daughtering prize. The scores are _not_ meant to induce bragging (or blaming). This quiz is simply a tool for introspection and sharing with others about the work taking place in your relationships and what is required to maintain flourishing families. Remember, there is no one-size-fits-all approach to family life. Hopefully, you have noticed or appreciated something new about daughtering from this chapter and quiz that can make an impact on your perspective and your relationships.

Chapter 2

WHAT IS A GOOD DAUGHTER?

THE SOCIAL LANDSCAPE

I was sitting with Diem and she started to get a bit emotional when she was telling me about watching a friend get married. Diem said, "I watched all morning as she got her hair and makeup done and got dressed. Her mom was there, flitting in and out of the room, saying supportive stuff. Her mom was just so present. And she included her mom in everything, even making sure the stylist did her mom's hair just right." Diem went on to share more details from that day as she had watched them interacting and how it made her feel.

From that experience, Diem crafted a plan to have her mom involved on her wedding day. Even though Diem didn't share the same level of closeness with her mom, she noticed how special and important it was to mark that big milestone together. It's a classic daughterhood experience women have: watching their friends do daughtering and then adopting or adjusting it for their own life.

Daughterhood refers to the collective experience shared by adult daughters, each navigating unique circumstances but recognizing commonality in the way you fulfill your role. Similar to the term *sisterhood*, daughterhood emphasizes communal bonds, shared wisdom, and mutual support. Daughterhood is uniquely tied to the condition of being someone's daughter.

Differently, the state of *motherhood* is tied to being a mom, but also clearly demarcated by an irreversible transition into the role when you expand your family with a child. *Womanhood* encompasses all these situations, serving as the broadest category that includes daughterhood, sisterhood, and motherhood, each reflecting specific aspects of women's identities and experiences.

Importantly, daughterhood doesn't arrive with a singular event but is enduring from birth to death. Once into adulthood, daughters can reflect how they have come to know their daughtering role. Though no one sat you down for a class or lesson, you have learned to do daughtering not only through your personal relationships but by observing, relating to, and learning from other women. Be it friends, sisters, or even fictional characters, daughters are sponges, gathering knowledge for our roles and redefining with each new bit of information collected. That is, your daughtering is situated in time, culture, and relationships, not existing as an isolated or as a singular experience. When you embrace daughterhood as a communal phenomenon, you can better navigate societal expectations, find happiness in your role, and define daughtering on your own terms.

WHY DEFINE DAUGHTERING AS A FORM OF LABOR?

When it comes to daughters and their role in families, there are many words you could use to define and describe their behaviors and interactions, and each of these choices is poignant and important. So, why call daughtering a form of *labor*, when you could call it something else? (A privilege? A right? An obligation? Typical family interaction?)

Organizational researchers define work as a socially situated endeavor rooted in relationships, performed by people to meet needs for survival as well as higher-order needs such as social contribution, interpersonal connection, and self-determination. This definition includes marketplace (paid) employment and family labor, but most important it allows us to think of work through social and relational perspectives. For years, scholars have cited concerns with the ways women's labor is misunderstood and misused in society. Care and caring behaviors provided by women often go uncredited as labor, but the toll daughtering takes on women has emotional, financial, and physical impacts.

Thinking of daughtering as real, valuable work helps us appreciate the hidden contributions women make to their families and society. Subtle, frequent daughtering adds up, cumulatively requiring your considerable time, energy, and emotional resources. These little bits of daughtering here and there impact your ability to fully engage in other areas of your life. Recognizing small yet persistent acts as labor brings attention to the personal costs involved in caring, reminding us just how essential and impactful your daughtering can be.

When you start treating (and talking about) daughtering as actual labor, you open the door to assigning it a monetary value. Conceptualizing daughtering as labor enables an economic valuation through methods like estimating "shadow wages," the theoretical cost if someone else performed these tasks.

You could theoretically pay someone else to help your dad figure out his iPhone or even keep him company while watching the big game, but there's also an opportunity to enjoy your work. While the emotional dimension of doing daughtering with some of the most special people in your life makes it a bit more complicated than working the counter at the smoothie place, many forms of daughtering offer benefits, even while taking up your time, as you get satisfaction from being around your family or fulfilling a role that you were born into.

These complicating factors make it tricky to measure the true worth of daughtering in dollars and cents. Women don't want to outsource the good parts of being in a family. Nonetheless, every minute of our time is valuable. Placing a monetary value on daughtering can help society better recognize and appreciate the significant role women play through these quiet, everyday acts. Framing daughtering economically underscores its tangible worth and highlights the broader implications of women's invisible labor within family and societal structures. Plus, employers and policymakers are more likely to understand dollars and cents when creating leave policies and benefits programs.

More than a calculation or amount of money, though, the goal here is to demonstrate that a woman's contribution to society *matters*. *Mattering* is a powerful psychological concept. Mattering represents social integration and inferred significance, aka, people care about the thing. If daughtering matters to the world, to society, that's enough for a lot of women. You may not be looking for your daughtering job to be substituted out, changed, lessened, or paid for. But you may yearn to be seen and have your contributions matter.

Acknowledging daughtering is so much more than giving a woman a pat on the back. It's about understanding the longstanding losses of time, energy, effort, and freedom that women are saddled with over men. All because we think of doing daughtering as "family stuff" and not "real work." And yet, it feels very real to the women doing it.

THE LIMINALITY OF DAUGHTERHOOD

Being a daughter and part of the collective experience of daughterhood can feel like you're living in a liminal space—a place where you're not quite here or there, a threshold where you are often transitioning from one state to another. For instance, imagine the feeling you have when you're about to hit a milestone birthday, but the big day hasn't quite come yet. Or, once that big birthday has come and gone, you may not feel much different, at least not right away. Birthdays are a kind of liminal, transitory space where something is shifting, but it's hard to pin down exactly what changes and when it happens. In fact, the word *liminal* comes from the Latin word, *limen*, meaning threshold.

For daughters, liminality can mean having that feeling of being in flux, where your role and identity are fluid, and always evolving, despite having always been and persisting into the future with some sense of certainty. You can recall your entire past, while also holding on to dreams for your future. You're moving between expectations from your family, society, and even yourself, taking it all in and trying to make sense of it. The process of figuring out how to meet all these demands without losing your sense of self is never really over. In the liminal space of daughterhood, you're never quite sure if you're doing it "right," if you're good enough, or if you're ever going to get closer to that ideal of what a daughter should be.

Understanding the liminality of daughterhood matters because it reveals the invisible, nuanced emotional and psychological spaces that daughters live in. Thinking about daughtering as an "in-between" metaphysical space isn't just a poetic thought exercise; it is essential. When you embrace your liminal experiences, the complexities and the ineffable nature of daughtering can coalesce into a knowing. With that new self-assurance, you can claim your "good daughtering," even as it evolves.

Take Bianca, age 31, who comes from a big Mexican American family who love to travel. As one of four daughters, Bianca learned the value of togetherness early on. In her words, "Family is something we value, that we hold dear to our hearts." Her closeness with her parents, sisters, and extended family is central to her identity, and living away from them after moving for work is a bittersweet part of her life.

But her sense of responsibility also comes with challenges, especially when the pressures of modern life collide with the traditions. Family travel is one of Bianca's liminal spaces where she navigates both work and fun while doing daughtering.

Bianca has become the default, designated "flight-getter." She told me that it can be a burden to organize flights for seven people, reserved on her credit card, while also trying to negotiate the PTO needed for the trip. And she doesn't get reimbursed by her family for the flights. "It's alright. My dad pays for the hotels, so it all kind of works out," she tells me. Bianca relays that she's not bothered by paying more and spending the money on her family, because she is glad she can do this for the family.

Bianca admits it's a balancing act to meet the expectations of family and the demands of her career, but she says this without pessimism because she truly enjoys family time. Bianca has a strong sense of responsibility, and she's keenly aware of the support needed by her parents, both emotionally and financially.

Many intangible daughtering behaviors exist only inside a woman's brain or in the tangible text message threads of her telephone. And some forms of daughtering are only inside our identities and remain nearly untraceable unless we chase them down. These spaces are particularly difficult to access, and to describe.

One daughter, Nita, told me about a liminal space that she occupies. She sees herself as a bridge to generations past, going back to her great-grandmother, who was a refugee forced to flee her country. Passed down from woman to woman in her family, Nita feels a connection to the pain of their collective story, but also to their resilience. Each generation bore this invisible weight—trauma mingled with pride. Nita has carried it silently within herself, an act of daughtering unseen by others but profoundly felt.

Scholar Kerry Daly suggested we can better understand the dynamics of families by borrowing from the art world's metaphor of positive and negative spaces when thinking about everyday family life. *Positive spaces* are where forms are visible, and noticeable. The forms in positive spaces easily draw our eye when looking at art. In terms of families, this is like when family scholars look at conversations, fights, or rituals that are easily observable and can help us learn about behaviors that shape a family. But it is the negative spaces, according to Daly, that we are unaccustomed to looking at—but that doesn't make them any less important.

Negative space, in art or graphic design, is an area that recedes from notice, where it appears as if nothing exists between the obviously visible forms. Some might even call that space empty. But negative space is crucial for artists to harness, as the places that lack attention are often as important as those we are drawn to so easily. In terms of families, these are the areas that are overlooked, like the influence of spirituality, myth, and intuition. Daly emphasizes that families often carry implicit beliefs, rituals, and intuitive practices that are rarely articulated. These liminal spaces are nonetheless influential in women's daily lives. I think a lot of women can see themselves in the undefined and in-between world where daughtering is concerned.

Daughterhood Liminality and Time

How do we define success when being a daughter means different things to different people, and even to ourselves at various points in time? Hello, adolescence! Hello, new motherhood! Hello, perimenopause! The challenge is conceptualizing the daughtering experience when we're constantly adapting to new demands, even living inside new bodies and with a new cast of characters as people enter and exit our lives over a lifespan.

Aviva, 44, talked about how her father recently revealed that he was thinking of moving to town. For years, she had navigated her role as an adult daughter by keeping a comfortable emotional and physical distance from her dad, balancing occasional visits and polite conversations with the demands of what she called her "regular life." In recent months, however, her dad had begun hinting that he was struggling financially. Whenever that came up, Aviva said she stayed quiet, neither asking for more information nor offering to help. She really did not want to be financially involved. But she still felt the impending nature of the unasked request.

Aviva felt the weight of the new expectations pressing on her. While she had been comfortable with their familiar repartee, now her dad and his issues were pressing in uncomfortably close. She hadn't come to a resolution yet on what she might need to do for her father. Even the thinking work (anticipation or dread?) of preparing for a future conversation drained her emotional reserves. And yet Aviva was glad to be a stable person in her dad's life. Often the only constancy of daughterhood is change and the liminality of the routines and dynamics we put in place with our parents. Aviva was experiencing one of the consistencies of daughterhood: its changing nature is undefined, liminal, and even negative or anticipatory spaces.

Liminality of Daughterhood and Happiness

As a daughter, happiness is often fluid, defined not just by our personal satisfaction but by how well we meet the needs of others. Other times, it's about our own sense of accomplishment or feeling of peace in navigating this complex role well.

In the bestselling book *The Happiness Project*, author Gretchen Rubin details her own systematic approach to finding a little bit more happiness across several areas of her life. But the part that got my attention is when Rubin describes happiness as an ongoing process with no end point. While Rubin discovered a few happiness-boosting methods that worked for her, the key takeaway from her book is that, while there may be similarities where we agree on what creates happiness, each of us must find our own version of it—and seeking happiness is a process that is ongoing.

As I read, I thought about liminality, or the experience of standing on the threshold, where happiness can seem like it's just out of reach. There's a sense of agency, anticipation, and continuation that keeps us pursuing that transformative experience. Happiness isn't a destination. It shifts with time, experience, and the evolving expectations we hold for ourselves and others. The pursuit of positive experiences creates a hopeful anticipation that sustains us.

As daughters, we must think beyond the goal of achieving a singular definition of happiness. We pause and adjust and reimagine daughtering and daughterhood at each new stage of life.

I think there's a kind of fulfillment in the act of reaching toward the threshold in the pursuit of more, even though it may not come easily. There's satisfaction in the growth and journey.

But the problem with the liminality of daughtering is that it can leave us feeling unanchored, uncertain, and constantly questioning ourselves. In a liminal space, the idea of success is vague, with no fixed point to aim for. This uncertainty is emotionally exhausting because you're left wondering if you're doing enough, if you're meeting expectations, or if you even understand what those expectations are. You may even wonder if you're good enough, and is all this ever going to make you happy.

WHAT DOES IT ACTUALLY MEAN TO BE "GOOD"?

I conducted a study asking women what makes a "good" daughter and allowed them to determine the guidelines for what it means to be "good" for themselves. My research partner and I wanted to know more about how adult daughters construct their roles within families, but as we did the interviews, we were surprised to learn that women are giving themselves a self-assessment—like a grade for their daughtering—based on how they've come to understand what it means to be "good."

Before answering questions about what they actually do, the daughters we interviewed were priming us to their understanding of what they *should* do. These women were telling us what "good" daughters do—but then also grading themselves on whether they lived up to these expectations.

We analyzed the data and found four key themes related to women's perceptions of being good daughters: respect, protection, connection, and invitation. Respect meant the ways daughters interacted with their parent; protection was about safeguarding their parents emotionally and physically; connection described building and maintaining meaningful bonds; and invitation referred to daughters' openness to reciprocal nurturing.

The women in this study identified these expectations for being a good daughter as coming from their moms and other socialized messages received as they were growing up. Sometimes, daughters claimed, they were able to achieve the expected level of daughtering. Other times, however, the daughters felt they were not measuring up.

We sorted these responses into two main categories—ones that society would typically see as acceptable for adult daughters, and ones that wouldn't quite meet those expectations. When women felt like they weren't measuring up to the idea of being a "good daughter," it often led them to reflect on their role in a personal way. We grouped those self-reflections into two more categories: ones that helped them move forward (productive) and ones that held them back (destructive).

We looked at how adult daughters think about what "good" daughters are "supposed" to do and how that matches up with the ways they feel about doing it. We mapped four types: Some women are doing what they think they should and it works well for them—this is the socially ideal "good daughter" space. Others are doing what's expected but feel drained and unhappy. Then there are women who *aren't* doing what's expected and feel bad about it—like they're letting people down. And finally, some are breaking the mold, doing less than what's considered "enough," but they're actually okay with that and feel good about their choices.

What surprised my colleague and I was how many daughters feel unsatisfied but keep doing daughtering anyway—because it's expected, and because they expect it of themselves. This study made me realize that I needed to spread the message that the point isn't just to ask whether you're doing enough, it's also to ask if the way you're doing daughtering is working for *you*.

WHAT DOES IT MEAN TO BE "HAPPY"?

The question of happiness is an important one; it's timeless and may never be answered satisfactorily. But the question of what makes *you* happy calls for you to ask yourself what you want, what you like, and how you can fulfill those desires. Some scholars, particularly from the field of positive psychology, set about studying this deep philosophical question in a methodical, scientific way, including Dr. Martin Seligman who began publishing meaningful research in the late 1990s, focusing his happiness inquiries on finding ways to improve well-being through the pursuit of meaningful relationships. Seligman shifted his focus from traditional psychology, which often emphasized diagnosing and treating illness and disorders, to exploring what makes life worth living. Seligman authored pioneering academic and popular texts about happiness and how individuals can cultivate a fulfilling life. He organizes life's happinesses into the categories of hedonic and eudaemonic impacts.

Hedonic happiness refers to the pursuit of pleasure, comfort, and immediate gratification. This is the happiness of now. Hedonic forms of happiness include activities that provide quick excitement or sensory pleasure, such as enjoying a good meal, drinking and dancing into the night, or blowing a bunch of money on a day at the carnival.

In the context of family relationships, hedonic happiness can be seen in shared moments like a fun family outing or laughing over a cup of coffee at the breakfast table. These hedonic happiness moments are like snapshots. In your mind's eye, you can picture past instances of hedonic enjoyment when you were filled with good feelings about your mom or dad, when you were uplifted and giggling, or feeling a thrill at sharing a juicy bit of family gossip.

You can also imagine future moments of hedonic happiness, like enjoying a fun card game or the fun of a thrift-store hunt. Mary, a 51-year-old daughter, told me that she and her mom like to go out to eat together, trying new foods and restaurants. And Alexis, a 39-year-old daughter, told me that she always takes her dog when she visits her parents. Her dad gives the dog a lot of love and attention, which both Alexis and the pup enjoy. Hedonic happiness experiences with family are easily recognizable and don't have to be as exciting as winning the lottery to count as moments of pleasure.

Eudaemonic happiness, on the other hand, is a type of pleasure found in living a life of purpose and meaning, often associated with personal growth and being your best self. This type of happiness is about contributing to something lifelong and sustainable. Eudaemonic happiness is about knowing you will like yourself tomorrow, no matter what hijinks you get into today. When you think of eudaemonic happiness that comes from relationships and connection, it is built over many experiences and over many days and hours.

Within a family, eudaemonic happiness might come from the satisfaction of providing monetary support to parents, resolving conflicts in a reasonable way, and being proud of yourself as a daughter. These results are built over time little by little. Eudaemonic happiness may not always provide that dopamine hit of pleasure but is found instead in the times when you are effectively "adulting." Eudaemonia contributes to a deeper sense of well-being and connection over time, when you feel satisfied that you have done a good job over the long haul and tried everything possible to create a lasting impact.

As you can imagine, there are a lot of family experiences where hedonic and eudaemonic happiness overlap. Going on a walk with your parent can serve for both enjoyment in the moment and also offering a lasting sense of satisfaction that you contributed to both your and your parent's health and longevity. But these two types of happiness may occasionally be at odds. Take, for example, Jamie, a 24-year-old daughter who described to me how when she argues with her mom, her mother gets frustrated and starts lecturing her, even though she is an adult. Does Jamie want to hear these things or think she deserves the lecture? No. "But I would never tell my mother I don't want to hear it. Never," Jamie said emphatically. There's a trade-off here. In Jamie's argument with her mom, the trade-off is respecting her mother, while walking away and feeling like she was a considerate daughter for not arguing. The eudaemonic happiness of showing respect is worth more to Jamie than winning an argument and experiencing the hedonic happiness of being right.

In another example, Jimena, a 31-year-old daughter, told me that some daughtering things aren't very pleasurable for her, but neither do they cost her very much, so she does them anyway. Though Jimena is not religious, whenever she visits her parents, she attends Catholic mass with them. Why? It makes them feel good, which makes her feel good, eudaemonically. For Jimena, the church service doesn't give her the hedonic pleasure of doing something fun like getting a nice coffee and reading the paper on a Sunday morning might do, but it serves another important purpose. Though she knows that her parents want more religious talk and action from Jimena, she draws a line that she'll do no more than attend a service with them.

Sometimes, daughters can and do prioritize their hedonic happiness. One daughter, Brooke, age 26, told me that she knows her mother would like more phone calls. Brooke admitted that she would like to call her mother more, too, if that means making her mom happy, but it just doesn't seem possible right now. Brooke's time is limited and some days she just doesn't have the energy to call. She prioritizes the other things she needs in her day, like friendships or relaxing alone. Even though she has identified her mom's need and would like to meet it, Brooke is also facing the reality of each day without guilt or burden. And if that means grabbing a glass of wine and taking a long soak in the tub instead of calling Mom, Brooke makes that choice.

Each of us has to make trade-offs between hedonic and eudaemonic happiness, while recognizing that these decisions have consequences for ourselves and others. Seligman's work emphasizes the importance of balancing both hedonic and eudaemonic pursuits of happiness to achieve a well-rounded and fulfilling life. We need some of each. Sometimes we need to act out of the momentary pursuit of pleasure in front of us. And other times, we need to avoid the spontaneous pleasures in order to act in the interests of our and our parents' lifelong happiness.

Seligman's research revealed that individuals who engage in meaningful activities, particularly within family settings, tend to experience greater overall life satisfaction than those who solely pursue pleasure. Daughters, it seems, are exceptional at pursuing the sort of happiness that contributes to lifelong happiness within their families. You might even feel it at your core and pursue this family flourishing without knowing how to identify the impact it will have on your own happiness. What brings you daughtering delight? Is it the heartfelt conversations or renovating a kitchen together? Or perhaps some of both?

B+ DAUGHTERING

If you were earning a grade for doing daughtering, I would like to suggest that a B+ would signify a satisfactory performance with adequate effort. Landing you somewhere around 88 percent of perfection, this paradigm is one I have long used myself. There are many days where I am a B+ daughter and proud of it. I leave text messages unread and unanswered. I forget to bite my tongue. And I don't always put my dish in the dishwasher at my parents' house. But I did give an excellent hug, listen attentively during the last call, and kept the grandkids alive this week. Life is about balance, and I must compel myself to notice when my daughtering is "good enough" and quit there.

Being a "good enough" adult daughter isn't about trying to be perfect. Perfection has never been the goal, nor is it an attainable goal line. This idea of "good enough" comes from pediatrician and psychoanalyst Donald Winnicott's concept of "good enough" mothering, the argument that moms don't have to be flawless to raise happy, secure kids. And while Winnicott liked to help mothers improve their parenting and build strong relationships with their babies, he also noticed a tendency in new mothers to be very hard on themselves and aim for perfection.

The same goes for daughters—being "good enough" means providing care and support in a way that feels right, without trying to meet impossible standards. Daughtering is about finding that balance where you're there for your family, but not at the expense of what's best for you.

Daughters can find themselves striving to make every inter-action with their parents the very best it can be, but that level of perfectionism isn't sustainable. Trying so hard to be a wonderful daughter all the time can create feelings that you're *never* enough *any of the time*. Rather than a focus on what she's doing well, the daughter who is trying to do *everything* right will notice the tiniest of flaws in herself. *Am I calling Dad enough? Should I visit more? Was my tone too harsh on the phone?* Doing B+ daughtering leaves room for self-care and flexibility, which ultimately helps you stay more present and grounded in your relationships.

But what about the gap that's left when a daughter gets it wrong or doesn't get to the goal line? Remember, imperfection is not neglect. Daughters who leave some tasks unfinished or cannot meet their parents needs immediately can rest assured that they are only human, and they have limits. Their parents (and siblings, spouses, children, and others) will adapt to fill in the other mo-ments of need. And daughters have to trust that parents can also find their own solutions to the small things in life because they are autonomous adults. There is no need for daughters to infantilize their parents, and plus, we cannot do it all: be mediator, emotional supporter, cheerleader, logistics coordinator, event planner, legal and tax expert, etc. Instead, we can focus on the things we do well and delegate the rest.

But what about when Mom starts the guilt trip that you're "never there" or "don't care anymore"? That's the time to stretch yourself in new ways by recognizing that these changes can cause discomfort, but that doesn't make them wrong. Disappointing your parent may be awkward but it doesn't make you a bad daughter or mean that you have to go back to the way you were doing things before. The next time you experience a parental guilt trip, you can try affirming the relationship without giving up your boundary. That might sound like saying, "While I love spending time with you, I'm not available on that Saturday."

Guilt can sneak in the door if given the tiniest inch of space, but women can recognize that not every emotion is a valid one. Grab that guilt, look at it, and then let it go and watch it float away. It was there and now it's gone. Sometimes it helps to debrief with a friend or a therapist how you have handled some recent guilt trips. When you experience the strain of the adult daughter role, it can be helpful to have other wise people affirm that you handled it well.

A while back I bought my husband a T-shirt that said "World's Okayest Husband" as a gentle tease. This good man laughed and got the joke; he's a good husband and father for our family, though imperfect. Then he wore his tee proudly. Today I went back online to search and, sure enough, you can find "World's Okayest Daughter" tees to purchase. Maybe I'll go grab one for myself. You can be the "okayest," B+ daughter out there. Nothing more is needed.

The image of what a daughter "should" be is often shaped by cultural myths and societal narratives—ideas we may have absorbed without even realizing it. The challenge is in naming and understanding this experience when the lines are blurred between what's expected, what we can give, and how we measure success in such an ever-evolving role.

It's a liminal space of uncertainty and growth, where we navigate emotional complexity while trying to make sense of our place in our family and the world. Being part of this daughterhood—this collective experience of women doing daughtering—is an ongoing process of growth, transformation, and renegotiation. But understanding this broader scope helps us recognize the real work daughters do, which is often unacknowledged but nonetheless deeply impactful. The next step is to redefine what it means to be a daughter on our own terms.

ACTIVITY 2: IS YOUR DAUGHTERING FUNCTIONAL?

Let's explore how you see yourself as a daughter—and how your daughtering fits into your life. Here we will examine your perception of the right amount of daughtering and whether your current daughtering is functional for you in a three-step quiz. Daughtering that's functional is both useful and practical; it makes sense for you in your life. In the following three-step process, you will score your perceptions of daughtering, availability for doing daughtering, and identify your current daughtering paradigm.

Step 1: The first step is to evaluate your perceptions of daughtering. Ask yourself: Am I daughtering the way society expects a daughter to do daughtering? Am I doing what my mother expects? What do I expect of myself as an adult daughter?

For each question below, circle your response. On a scale from 1 to 5, respond to the prompts.

Add up your scores and check the scoring below.

Activity: Is Your Daughtering Functional? Step 1

DAUGHTERING PERCEPTIONS				

SOCIETY: How much do you feel you align with society's expectations of a "good" daughter?

1	2	3	4	5
Not at all				Completely

PRESSURE: How often do you feel pressure to do more for your parent than you currently do?

1	2	3	4	5
Always				Never

BOUNDARIES: How clear are your personal boundaries when it comes to helping or supporting your parent?

1	2	3	4	5
Not Clear				Very Clear

BALANCE: How well do you balance your own needs with the demands of daughtering?

1	2	3	4	5
Very Poorly				Very Well

INVOLVEMENT: When reflecting on your role as a daughter, how satisfied are you with your current level of involvement?

1	2	3	4	5
Not at all satisfied				Completely Satisfied

SCORING

16–25 points = Confident and Content

You are confident in the balance you've achieved as an adult daughter. You've likely set clear boundaries and feel at peace with your level of involvement. You don't feel external pressure to do more and have found a healthy balance between your own needs and the expectations of others. Your sense of satisfaction suggests that you believe you're fulfilling your role to the best of your ability and don't feel compelled by societal or personal guilt to increase your involvement.

5–15 points = Overburdened by "Shoulds"

You likely feel a significant amount of pressure—whether from society, your mother, or yourself—to do more in your daughtering role. This sense of obligation might leave you feeling overwhelmed or guilty, and you may often question whether you're doing enough. It's possible that you struggle with setting or maintaining boundaries, and you may prioritize your mother's needs at the expense of your own well-being. Your score indicates that you're likely feeling overburdened by the weight of these expectations.

Step 2: The next step is to evaluate your availability for doing daughtering. This will indicate whether the daughtering you are doing is functionally productive in your life, or if you are becoming burned out so much that daughtering is destructive. Ask yourself: Is doing daughtering functional in my life and do I have balance?

For each question below, circle your response. Add up your scores and check the scoring below.

Activity: Is Your Daughtering Functional? Step 2

DAUGHTERING AVAILABILITY				

TIME MANAGEMENT: How much time do you have to accomplish your personal responsibilities? How are you giving energy toward your family and doing daughtering?

1	2	3	4	5
Almost Never				Almost Always

EMOTIONS: Do you often feel overwhelmed by the amount of daughtering you are responsible for?

1	2	3	4	5
Almost Never				Almost Always

FAMILY AND PERSONAL LIFE BALANCE: Do you struggle to find time for hobbies, relaxation, or self-care because of your family's pull on your resources?

1	2	3	4	5
Almost Never				Almost Always

SUPPORT: Do you feel like you give more energy to your parent(s) than you receive in return?

1	2	3	4	5
Almost Never				Almost Always

REST: Do you have trouble sleeping or feel exhausted because of family concerns?

1	2	3	4	5
Almost Never				Almost Always

SCORING

5–15 points = Balanced and Busy

Your burnout level is low to moderate. You maintain a solid balance between daughtering responsibilities and other areas of your life. While daughtering is a significant part of your routine, it doesn't overwhelm you. You have managed to integrate this role in a way that allows you to maintain your well-being and energy. You effectively allocate your time and resources, ensuring that daughtering remains functional without causing undue stress. Overall, you are content with the balance you've achieved and feel in control of your responsibilities.

16–25 points = Drained Dry

Your burnout level is quite high. You may be experiencing significant stress and imbalance due to the demands of daughtering. This level of involvement might be leading to feelings of exhaustion and dissatisfaction. The pressure and effort involved in managing these responsibilities might be leaving you feeling drained and unhappy. It's crucial to evaluate how this intense level of daughtering is affecting your life and to seek ways to alleviate some of the strain, whether by setting boundaries, seeking additional support, or reevaluating your commitments.

Step 3: Now, let's put it together. Based on your perceptions and availability scores, you can evaluate whether you think you are doing what you ought to be doing as a daughter and whether it is functional daughtering that fits into your life.

When we put the scores from Steps 1 and 2 together, we can map these onto the quadrants from the research study to see how you evaluate your own "good daughtering."

Grounded Giver: Doing the daughtering I should (meeting expectations)/It's functional for me (balanced)
  • Confident & Contented + Balanced & Busy
Depleted Doer: Doing the daughtering I should (meeting expectations)/It's dysfunctional (burned out)
  • Confident & Contented + Drained Dry
Measured Mover: Not doing the daughtering I should (missing expectations)/It's still functional (balanced)
  • Overburdened by "Shoulds" + Balanced & Busy
Stretched Struggler: Not doing the daughtering I should (missing expectations)/It feels dysfunctional (burned out)
  • Overburdened by "Shoulds" + Drained Dry

These four classifications reveal the tensions daughters feel between the pull of doing daughtering duty and living their best lives. So, what is the value in knowing and understanding this about your daughtering? It contextualizes the experience of what it means to be a "good daughter." As you evaluate where you're currently at with your daughtering, it gives you some idea about how you might want to change and grow. You are noticing where expectations for daughtering come from and how they fit into your life. Keep reading to learn more about what you can change to make daughtering fit into your life in just the right ways.

Chapter 3

A DIFFERENT KIND OF DAUGHTER

HOW DO I REDEFINE MY ADULT DAUGHTER ROLE?

I opened Zoom and let Danni into the call, getting ready to start our interview. Prior to our chat, Danni filled out a questionnaire and read over her rights as a participant in a research study. Part of this document also includes an overview of the topics we will cover.

When we get on the video call together, I make a little speech about how all answers are good and helpful, so she should feel free to be open and honest. Danni then did what so many participants do—she warned me: "Well I hope I don't disappoint you, but I'm really not the right kind of daughter to talk to." This has happened so many times, where the woman basically tells me I've got the wrong gal. They laugh a little, but there's also some hesitancy. You see, these women are letting me in on their subversive secret that they're doing daughtering all wrong. According to her parents or a sibling, or maybe society, or herself, she's not the model daughter we should follow.

But how can it be that so many women are certain they are the wrong kind of daughter? They think that there's nothing I can learn from them. And they believe they are the minority—unsuitable and ill-fitting for the role. Other daughters, they're sure, are doing it *right*.

But little do these women realize that this kind of priming only reassures me that I do indeed have the right gal. This woman has a story and something to say that the typical daughter can learn from, and it's clear that they intend to tell me the truth in our interview rather than making up a fairy-tale account of a perfect fantasy daughter.

So, I smile at Danni and reassure her that I never have been interested in the perfect people because I can't relate to them. I'm not a perfect daughter and that's what we share in common. There is no way to be perfect, but we keep feeling as though there is. But how do daughters, like me and Danni, get the wrong idea about how to be the right kind of daughter?

WHAT'S REAL?
SOCIAL CONSTRUCTION OF OUR REALITIES

From an early age, individuals gather and organize fragments of life experiences into frameworks that guide their understanding of these roles. Much like building a house, these pieces come together to form a broader understanding of what it means to take on roles within a family. This creation of meaning making via life experiences is called *social construction*. Social constructionism explains how individuals create meaning and knowledge through a dynamic process of combining personal experiences, cultural narratives, societal norms, and interpersonal exchanges. This approach helps us understand how roles like grandmother, mother, father, sister, or daughter take shape.

Families communicating together are not merely a means of exchanging information but a fundamental way in which our social realities are shaped. Sociologists Peter Berger and Thomas Luckmann's seminal work, *The Social Construction of Reality*, outlines how we continuously interpret and assign meaning to others' actions, creating shared realities. For example, observing a smile from our dad as he tells a story about his workday may lead us to infer kindness or sarcasm.

Over time, we create meaning about the messages people are trying to convey with their bodies and their words. Children are excellent at reading the body language of parents and adults because they hold so much power over their lives. These observations slowly become patterns. And these patterns guide how individuals interact within roles, like mother and daughter, shaping behavior and expectations based on accumulated knowledge and experience.

Social roles are not static; they change based on how they are used and who is portraying them, and roles are cocreated through interaction. Mothers and daughters, for instance, collaboratively define their roles by imagining and responding to the expectations of the other. Role-making is an iterative, or self-reinforcing, process that relies on shared understandings built through communication. In short, you have to be there to see it.

I remember once when my mother and I went to visit my grandmother, who was in the hospital at the time, and we arrived a bit later than anticipated. We walked into the room and my grandmother greeted us and we went on to have a pleasant visit. Later, as I headed back to the car with my mom, she said to me, "Oh, I was in *so* much trouble when we got here late today." I looked at her, confused. Had we been in the same interaction? I asked her what she meant. And she said, "My mama gave me a look and I knew that she was angry we were late and hadn't called." I was so surprised. My grandmother angry? She had seemed normal to me, even pleasant. But that's the thing about body language and "looks" that mothers give their children. They are not shared by the whole world, but the key players always know what they mean.

My mom *knew* her mom was angry. Then, my grandmother masked her emotions and got on with the visit, probably because I was there. She put on a good show and put the anger to the side. I have thought about that interaction many times in the years since.

Did my grandmother's anger go away after a few minutes or did she just stuff it down inside? Did the two of them talk about it later, with my mom getting an earful during a phone call? I never found out.

Role-making is influenced not only by family dynamics but also by broader cultural and societal discourses, which intertwine individual and collective perspectives. I think of that classic Folger's coffee commercial from a few decades ago that features a brother and sister. They share a quiet cup of coffee together in the kitchen when he makes a surprise visit to the family home during the holidays. Why do I remember that commercial? Because I didn't have a brother growing up, so that dynamic fascinated me.

Now that I have a son and daughter myself, I am still waiting for the miraculous coffee that will trigger such a shared moment of love. (Maybe it will still come one day?!) But without my own formative experience with a brother, I was relying on the media to tell me what it was like. And a lot of us do that with roles with which we are unfamiliar or even with those roles we do play. We allow outside influences to shape how we act and react to our roles, because that's how we *think* it's done.

Even I tend to fall victim to watching overly sentimental Hallmark movies with idyllic mothers and daughters, then applying that same benchmark to myself and finding I keep coming up short. Based on what I see on TV and in movies, I can feel like I'm failing at daughtering miserably—and I certainly know better. But society, media, friends, and family can all influence how we think of our roles.

What's important about this discussion of social construction is to realize just how we got here: "here" being the place you're at right now as a daughter. You got here by having a lot of building blocks that led you to your current understanding of how to be a daughter. And some of those building blocks are decades old. The oldest building blocks that create our experiences are both foundational for our understanding, but also, they are simply *old*. And sometimes the old stuff isn't quite as true anymore. The building blocks we have used to construct our roles together have served us well but are also subject to maintenance needs.

There are a few principles of social construction. First, every interaction is essential to human existence. That means each bit of communication we give and receive contributes to the ongoing formation of our roles and relationships; every single piece of information you've learned or been given about being a daughter is of value. And you have used all of it to get to where you are today.

Second, conversations we have as individuals reflect and reinforce larger societal norms. There's a reflexive relationship between the single human being and the larger social world. This means that you influence and are influenced *by* what you have heard about women, mothers, daughters, and relationships.

Third, when we recognize the constructed nature of our reality, then we can critically examine the societal assumptions that generally go unquestioned. By becoming aware of how the role of a daughter is cobbled together, you can now examine why and how it is so. You can see the mortar between the bricks of the house and question why it was made that way. And do you even like the way it's been put together?

And that's what brings us to this place: you, your thoughts and actions, and those of others before you and around you. We are daughters and the reason our daughtering remains invisible is because we have continued to agree to participate in a society that devalues our work. But we don't have to stay invisible. We can change the building materials and form a new pattern in the tilework.

Roles (and the identities that go with them) for motherhood and daughterhood are formed and re-formed through continuous dialogue, both within the family and in interactions with the wider world. That means talking—communicating about who we are and what we do.

By talking about and negotiating our roles, family members actively shape what it means to belong to a family. We agree to serve and belong to a family and fill the roles of family members. It's our choice. We, as daughters, act with agency in our families and we can also make a difference. We're living in a house that's still being built, and we can speak up to change the roofline or the patio or the décor as we see fit. This ongoing construction through discourse is how ideas about identity and behavior are developed, validated, and internalized. We grow the role of daughter, stamp it as true, and then become that role from the inside out.

After my interview with Danni, where I learned a lot of interesting nuggets about her life and what she really thinks about being an adult daughter, I was left to reflect on how we can get the "right kind of daughter" and "my way of doing daughtering" to better align. In short, how do I make the world see that I'm already doing good daughtering? Or, at the very least, allow me to accept it? The key is to think of daughtering as you never have before—and allow yourself to believe it.

Now that you've done a lot of noticing about your own daughtering, social daughtering, and considered ideas of "good" and "happy," it's time to redefine daughtering on your terms.

Ask yourself, what do I *want* out of my daughtering? Each of the following sections provides a new paradigm for your approach to daughtering, allowing you to consider how to cultivate daughtering and daughterhood in your own way.

Reflecting on Your Current Role

The first step to redefining daughtering is to take stock of what your daughtering currently looks like. I remember watching the movie *Interstellar,* which has a great example of a daughter redefining her relationship with her father in adulthood. There is emphasis on Newton's Third Law in the film; the main character says that to move forward, you have to leave something behind. The thing from the past will give you perspective to know how far you've come. While there are probably better ways to interpret Newton, it's a useful paradigm. So that's where we will start, too. Figure out where your daughtering is at today, so in the future you will be able to see how far you've advanced.

Consider the many messages you've received about daughtering throughout your life: from family expectations, media portrayals, and societal narratives that define what a "good daughter" should be. In the past, we have been hindered by a borrowed vocabulary for discussing daughtering. Without words to clearly articulate the invisible efforts daughters undertake, the true complexity and depth of our work remain hidden or undervalued. You've probably felt this lack of recognition at times, wondering if your efforts as a daughter even matter.

As you take stock of how you choose to do daughtering, you might see areas flourishing, full of interpersonal growth and healthy relationships. These aspects of your daughter role feel authentic, rewarding, and meaningful to you. But perhaps, you'll also identify some unwanted expectations, unhealthy communication patterns, or obligations that drain your emotional resources without replenishing them.

A student who I was mentoring, Mallory, age 21, sat with me and described her frustration with her dad. He called her a few days ago to check on her, and then added some unsolicited advice on her sleep and social schedule. Mallory was in her third year of college and did not appreciate her dad's suggestions. I empathized with her feelings and followed up with a few more questions, asking Mallory what she told her dad she was going to do about his advice. "Oh," Mallory said, "I didn't text back." Mallory hadn't responded to her dad's advice at all.

She went on to say that responding to her dad with any kind of disagreement could lead to an argument or a multiday silent treatment or even impact her finances, since she relied on her parents for a sizable portion of her budget. That led me to wonder how Mallory intended to solve this dilemma. Could she just leave things at odds with her dad or maintain silence? That wasn't an option for her, so she told me that she did half of what her dad told her to do and half of what she wanted to do. That proportion, according to Mallory, was enough to satisfy her dad and let her feel free from his rule.

Mallory said that she didn't pick up her dad's calls for two days but continued texting with him. Their communication seemed like a dance, or maybe a sparring match. One person steps forward, the other reacts by stepping back. One parries, the other feints. But they stay locked in sync. Mallory knew her dad wanted her to be safe, healthy, and successful. She wanted that for herself too, but with some independence. She either didn't have enough power to tell him to "buzz off" or she had decided it simply wasn't worth it to get locked in conflict with him. This tension in their communication, though disorganized, was working out okay for her.

Stories like Mallory's illustrate the subtleties involved in daughtering: There's an ongoing effort to balance self-identity and parental expectations. Yet this balance can feel strained, as you try to determine which parental expectations genuinely align with your values, and which ones feel imposed, unnecessary, or burdensome.

The first step toward redefining your daughter role involves clearly acknowledging any patterns you see, both positive and negative. Only then can you decide what to do moving forward. Awareness is the foundation from which your intentional daughtering can grow.

Clarifying Your Values and Daughtering Practices

Only after looking closely at your life and circumstances can you then ask yourself, *What do I want now?* For changes to your daughtering, start by taking a careful look at the inherited expectations, behaviors, and relational patterns that exist between you and your parent(s). And then ask yourself, what would change if you began actively strategizing a fresh result, with a clean slate?

As adult daughters, we can thoughtfully select the behaviors, values, and relational dynamics we want to increase and implement. You're not bound to continue the family dynamics you had before—society's expectations, familial patterns, or even your past self's priorities. Throughout my interviews, daughters expressed the importance of clearly defining their own priorities. Take Laney's story, for example. Now in her late 40s, Laney has consciously decided to cultivate a life that aligns with her own needs and desires rather than societal or familial pressures.

Laney has been a partner to her guy for two decades; they do not have children. After more than a decade of her mom asking her when the grandkids were coming along, Laney is finally grateful that the questions have stopped. "No, there will be no children," she says. Laney has never felt the urge to be a mom.

One of the biggest reasons she's glad her mom stopped asking is because it bothered Laney every time she heard the question. It made her feel like her mom was not satisfied with Laney's life choices. At least, that was the story she was telling herself. While her mother's questioning made her doubt herself, Laney finally chose to stop trying to please or fulfill her mom's expectations. Instead, she set clear boundaries and created emotional clarity about what she wanted out of life.

Laney has untangled some complicated emotions from her childhood, and she is quite content with her spouse and pups. As for her parents, she aims to visit them out of state once a year. She allots one phone call a week for each parent and dreads the day that they will need more help in their elderhood. Laney says she worries because she's the only female child in the family and is anxious about what the work will entail. But that's tomorrow's trouble, and for today, she is content with the amount of connection and distance she has established, quite firmly, in her family.

Laney's story illustrates how powerful and freeing intentionality can be. It's not always easy to choose something new, especially when others around you have a clear picture of what they think your life should be like. But the reward of growing something truly aligned with your values is deeply satisfying. And it was clear to me that Laney was deeply satisfied with her life, showing a kind of inner peace and self-possession that many women crave. Laney's story is one so many women are happily living—daughtering but not mothering.

You, too, can select new practices for your life. The choice is yours to determine what truly brings joy, meaning, or balance. Perhaps you value emotional closeness but not daily interactions, or maybe practical support resonates more than frequent social visits.

There is no universally "correct" set of daughtering values—only those that align best with your individual identity, your family's circumstances, and your own happiness.

Minding Your Family

Once you've determined the values and practices you want to enact with intentionality, you can begin to mind the relationship by evaluating the daughtering opportunities that pop up. You already have many of the tools you need to do daughtering, and this is your opportunity to apply them. *Minding*, according to the family sociologists John Harvey and Julia Omarzu, describes the thinking process involved in achieving closeness with another person in a long-term relationship. While Harvey and Omarzu discuss minding primarily in the context of romantic couples, they also say the theory can be applied to any long-term committed individuals in a close relationship. By paying attention to our relationship, we create a synergistic force that reinforces the importance of the relationship and produces further minding. Minding is a thought and activity pattern, they say, that is built into the day-to-day reality of a relationship.

For daughters, minding your relationship with your parent means paying attention to the connection you have, prioritizing its importance, and strategizing ways to improve closeness. Minding cannot be passive, where you sit back and simply observe your life and relationships as they happen. Instead, minding is the action of intentional thought with the goal of making a difference in your family life. Minding is just one example of the ways daughters can begin to amass the tools and resources needed, if lacking, to cultivate the family dynamics you want to see.

Take, for example, April, who told me that she schedules text messages and emails to her parents. Using the feature on her phone that allows her to send messages later at a selected date and time, she sometimes creates messages in batches and then plans when they should arrive. The same can be achieved by putting a note in your calendar to remind you to ask someone a follow-up question about an event in their life or set up a coffee chat. These strategies are designed to increase closeness, but it's not so bad if they also improve efficiency, too.

Daughters can also be aware of tending to their relationships with everyday tasks that add up to something important, even though they may seem very mundane. Tending includes everyday care provisions and acts of altruism for the benefit of the other person or the relationship. Psychologist Shelly Taylor described the tend-and-befriend effect she often observed in women in her studies. In times of stress, she noted, women's instincts are to first nurture or care for another in need and then seek cooperation from a community who can support them in this goal. The ways we tend and befriend someone in our family may not look, from the outside, quite like how a "classic" or "perfect" daughter might do them, but your actions still have worth. Whether you're giving someone care and support because you want to or just think you're supposed to, it still counts.

Consider Vickie, who initially saw herself as the "wrong" type of daughter. During our conversation, Vickie described herself as not fitting the stereotype of the emotionally nurturing daughter. She said, "Thank God for my sister. She does all the stuff with my mom that I don't want to do." Vickie's sister handled the daily phone calls, emotional bolstering, and inane chitchat—tasks Vickie appreciated but didn't enjoy personally. She had fallen into the trap of thinking that her kind of daughtering wasn't as valid as her sister's softer mode.

Yet Vickie played a different, equally crucial role in her family's relational ecosystem. After her dad passed away, Vickie took on all the complex logistical and financial tasks. She managed probate, handled complicated legal paperwork, paid the bills, and established financial security for her mom and sister. She told me, somewhat dismissively, "I'm just the paperwork daughter. Nothing special. I'm not the nice, sweet daughter."

As Vickie spoke, I saw how she undervalued her enormous contributions, mistakenly believing her type of daughtering wasn't good enough. Her work was done with quiet strength—steady, supportive, and a guard against the outside world. Without Vickie's diligent labor in her area of strength, the family wouldn't have a solid structure to depend upon. Vickie and her sister together represented a powerful balance: two daughters dividing tasks in the family based on their strengths and preferences. They were jointly tending the relationship with their mother, and with each other, as they completed tasks that suited their skills and demeanors. Remember, you don't have to be supersweet or provide daughtering within a narrow scope of acceptable behaviors to give yourself credit for doing daughtering. It *all* counts.

Another vital tool for effective daughtering is developing a deep appreciation for your own contributions, even if they don't align with traditional or popular definitions of "good daughtering." Your unique way of engaging with your family has value precisely because it fits who you are, what you love, and what you're good at. By valuing yourself, you are better primed to appreciate the benefits of being a daughter in a family.

Nurturing your identity as a good daughter through self-awareness and intentional self-care is fundamental. Your emotional and mental health forms the foundation for a balanced and sustainable daughtering role. But it's also true that learning how to take care of ourselves can get a bit messy. Like me, you may feel like taking time for yourself is not only challenging, but confusing. I find myself wondering, "What does effective rest look like?" Reflective practices, mindfulness, journaling, or even simply acknowledging your needs can all enrich your inner landscape and enhance your resilience.

Since I'm not very good at slowing down, I remind myself that self-care can also be fast-paced and upbeat. I can foster emotional health and a rich inner life through making silly dance videos, putting on my favorite makeup, or going out for cocktails with friends. Not only is the goal of these endeavors to make me feel better individually, but to create a fertile ground from which I can care for important others.

Lastly, adult daughters can actively build support systems and skill sets to help their relationship thrive. My friend Jill and I are great at "downloading and debriefing" our lives to each other; over voice memos or videos, we share the highs and lows. Just saying things out loud makes them easier to process. With my friend Tiffany, we share a long history together, so we can use a shorthand to describe our lives that I have with no one else. The benefit of doing daughtering, and life, with other women who see you is invaluable.

Vickie's story reminds us that each daughter needs different skills and a positive mindset to nurture ourselves and others in close relationships. Her strength was in providing critical support in practical matters, demonstrating that there are many valid ways to contribute to a flourishing family. And that's exactly what I told her. I couldn't leave the interview without assuring Vickie that her daughtering was necessary, important, and so helpful to her family. Those are the qualities of effective daughtering that help bond families together. When you acknowledge and value your unique daughtering gifts, skills, and limitations, you can truly thrive—beautifully, authentically, and on your terms.

Sibling Dynamics in Family Life

Although we have agency to shape our daughtering role, it doesn't exist in a vacuum. If you have siblings, you know that they significantly influence the family ecosystem we inhabit. Understanding sibling dynamics helps us recognize how these relationships affect our own role and behaviors as daughters.

You can think of siblings like colleagues in your relationship career. They join in on some of the work, but they have their own jobs to do, too. Some of them are helpful and fun but others are nearly intolerable. Siblings are as unique and different as any two individuals on the planet when it comes to personality and preferences. This reality sometimes makes it feel as though siblings had entirely different parents—even when raised in the same home.

Psychologist Dr. Gabor Maté has explained this clearly: Even siblings raised in the same house by the same parents don't actually experience the same parenting. Parents respond differently based on each child's temperament, gender, birth timing, and their own evolving relationship dynamics over time. One sibling might recall warmth from a parent, while another remembers strictness or emotional distance. Understanding these differences can be eye-opening and validating for siblings who share their stories and have them well received.

But this experience can also be explained through social construction. Each experience in our lives is a building block to our lived reality. Even when we have shared vacations, graduations, moves, and weddings with our siblings over the years, each person experienced the event differently, shaping their perspective of the world.

This explains why sibling accounts of family life may differ dramatically. It can also help explain why you struggle to understand why your sibling acts the way they do. Or why your parent treats them a certain way.

Recognizing, and even welcoming, sibling differences offers tremendous freedom. This level of flexibility can ease tensions between siblings who have differing views of their parents, allowing compassion rather than conflict to emerge. Accepting that your sibling's experience is as valid as your own can lead to deeper connections, less comparison, and greater peace within the family. Daughtering isn't a competition—it's a collective act, each sibling doing it in their own meaningful way.

Cutting the Noise—A Note on Birth Order

Understanding the influence of birth order on sibling relationships—and your own daughtering—requires caution. While theories like birth order provide interesting lenses for reflection, it's essential to approach them thoughtfully rather than treating them as absolute truths.

In recent years, the idea of birth order as a tool for predicting and explaining family relationships has regained popularity. Dr. Alfred Adler's early twentieth-century theories suggested birth order influenced personalities and family interactions in the following ways: eldest children as responsible leaders, middle children as negotiators or peacekeepers, youngest children as adaptable or adventurous, and only children as mature or independent from an early age.

Yet, contemporary research has consistently emphasized that birth order effects are rarely straightforward or predictive. The reality is far more complex. Birth order alone cannot determine how each daughter behaves or experiences her family relationships, because family dynamics involve countless intersecting factors, including culture, gender expectations, parental personalities, socioeconomic conditions, health, and individual temperaments.

Take my own relatives, for example. My mother was the middle of three daughters. Her eldest sister had significantly different memories of their father, who passed away when the girls were young, than their youngest sister, who had virtually no memory of him. Even though these siblings shared the same biological parents and many everyday happenings as part of their childhood, like going to church together, eating Sunday dinners, and traveling to see relatives on a road trip, each daughter was differently shaped by these events.

This is just one quick example of the limitations of simple birth-order explanations. My aunt crisply reminded my mother, "You didn't live with the Mom I lived with." Such statements highlight how birth order alone can't fully explain how family dynamics shape each individual's daughterhood experience. Nor has birth order been shown to be *predictive* in its ability to describe whether someone will make money, have a certain personality, or end up being the one to take care of their parents in later life.

While some studies have indicated patterns—such as older daughters assuming greater family responsibilities—it's critical to remember correlation does not equal causation. Daughters aren't simply products of birth order; they're actively shaped by the social construction over years of personal experiences, choices, and circumstances unique to each.

You might hear anecdotes from daughters passionately affirming birth order's impact—perhaps eldest daughters feeling responsible or youngest daughters feeling perpetually viewed as "the baby." These personal accounts can offer valuable insights. Yet as a researcher, I urge caution: Anecdotal experiences can be illuminating but shouldn't overshadow the complexities of family life. For instance, when some-one tells you about their horoscope being right or that they picked the winning lottery numbers that came to them in a dream, these things can be true at the individual level, while still failing to rise to the level of being a useful tool at the population level. Your birth order might inform how you've experienced daughtering, but it doesn't have to dictate your choices any more than you would assign meaning to other fallacious stereotypes—like women being better at childcare because of some natural instincts or proclivity for it.

And, since new research comes out all the time, perhaps there will come a time when we can make definitive conclusions about birth order's impact on families (I'm even working on some analyses myself). Ultimately, birth order theories that have been published so far are best used as lenses, not scripts. Feel free to explore them but remember to keep your personal agency at the forefront. Allow these ideas to spark self-awareness and understanding, but don't let them limit or define you.

Reshaping and Evolving

Psychologist Erik Erikson described how our roles and identities shift significantly over our lifespan, and this idea can be incredibly helpful when applied to daughtering. Each stage of adulthood—young adulthood, middle adulthood, and late adulthood—brings unique challenges and opportunities for reevaluating how we daughter. The key takeaways from Erikson's research that are relevant to the discussion of daughtering is the idea that people change over their lifetime, in generally similar ways to others, based on their social and biological development. You can give yourself permission to embrace the evolution of your daughtering as you age and change.

Young Adulthood (Ages 19–40)

Young adulthood is marked by individuation—developing your own identity apart from your parents while still maintaining a bond. So this period of young adulthood, according to Erikson, is characterized by both individuality and mutuality.

Many individuals attend college, move away from the family home, and explore their identities during this time. The push and pull of competing forces to separate but stay close make this stage challenging. But the time span of almost twenty years can cover quite a bit of living and change in a woman's life.

This process can create tension, as illustrated by Mallory's story earlier, where she balanced her independence against her father's advice, maintaining her autonomy through careful negotiation. Mallory was in a phase of development called *emerging adulthood* where the tug of independence battles with the magnetism of togetherness. The need to obey or respect one's parents (or at least avoid disagreement) is a hallmark of these early adult years, where individuation takes time to untangle.

Young adulthood begins with a launching from the parental nest. And as daughters launch, there are some big, rough transitions at times. The start of young adulthood can be startling, for both the newly "adult" child and their parent(s). But young adulthood doesn't end there. If you're in your 20s and 30s, this is your life stage.

In young adulthood, daughtering involves trying new things and eliminating aspects that don't serve you as you navigate the tension between independence and continued parental involvement. Some daughtering behaviors or traditions might feel restrictive at this stage, prompting you to selectively remove or alter them to create space for your own needs and identity. If you find that you can't keep up with every single family tradition you used to, like a Thanksgiving Turkey Trot or an Ugly Sweater Party because you're trying new events with other people, or if the multifamily group text is taking up too much of your time, cull them. You are still a member of the family even if you drop some rituals.

Middle Adulthood (Ages 40–65)

Middle adulthood, or midlife, is the time when adults are their most independent, career-minded, and busy selves, according to Erikson. Your life is crowded with responsibilities.

Women in this life stage are juggling balancing career, parenting, spousal, and community responsibilities. Daughters in this stage may have their own partners, are raising young children, and aspiring to move up the career ladder.

Career demands, family obligations, and caregiving roles can overwhelm your emotional and physical resources as daughters feel "sandwiched" between one generation and the next. This period of switching back and forth may not require changing diapers (of either generation), but it does pull a woman's time, energy, attention, and worry in multiple directions. The women you know in middle adulthood may be struggling just to make it through the day with all the demands on their resources.

Reyna told me that her parents were frequently asking to be included in their grandkids' lives, but the catch was that they wanted to do all the activities at their house. Reyna was in her early 40s, with a husband and two young kids, a job, a mortgage payment, and very little spare time. She told me that her mom considered this offer to be with the kids such a gift. But to Reyna, the "gift" came with the tags still on it: She had to do all the work to get the kids ready, drive over to their house, then try to keep all the precious breakable items safe during their visit, while keeping up humorous chitchat about her life the whole time. It was, in short, exhausting.

Yes, she loved her time with her parents. And yes, she was very happy to see Grandma and Papaw interacting with their grandchildren, so she considered it worth the effort. But it would be nice, just once, to be acknowledged for all the effort she goes through to make these "precious moments" spark to life. But Reyna tries to keep these thoughts to herself because she knows her folks would not understand her point of view. And they were definitely not going to change. Reyna navigates these demands skillfully but wishes for greater recognition of her efforts.

In middle adulthood, women become more sure of themselves, including their likes and dislikes. This translates to a certainty in interactions with their parents. Daughters know what they're willing to give and how much difficulty and conflict they can take from their family. Many set up their lives by simply living the way they enjoy, while others intentionally broach these subjects with parents by talking it out. In each life stage, family members must adjust to each other's new preferences and life circumstances.

Middle adulthood calls for intentionality: setting clear boundaries, being selective about commitments, and carefully managing resources like your energy and time. At this stage, clearly communicating your needs becomes crucial, ensuring your relationships grow sustainably.

Late Adulthood (Ages 65 and Onward)

Late adulthood, sometimes called elderhood, is the time that roughly correlates with the occurrence of career retirement and continuing into advanced age. In their elderhood, daughters face new realities. Careers end, health challenges may arise, and the reliance on extended family networks becomes more pronounced. According to Erikson, in late adulthood we reflect on our whole lives and come to terms with the unavoidable reality of death. While many women in this stage continue their daughtering with elderly parents in their 80s and 90s, still other women experience years without living parents.

My friend Sandra's dad recently passed away. He was in his late 80s. While Sandra's mom died more than three decades earlier, and she knew her dad's time was coming, she was not expecting the struggles to adjust to her new reality as a parentless daughter. For many years, Sandra, age 66, was the fulcrum for the family's events and gatherings, carrying on her mom's traditions for the rest of the group, which included four siblings, her dad, and his second wife. The family had one last big gathering a few weeks before he passed, and at this celebration she knew their time together was soon coming to an end, so she soaked up every moment with her dad and siblings together. She told me how much she misses her dad's phone calls and sometimes listens to some of his voicemail recordings. He would always say the exact same thing on each voicemail: "Helloooo, Sandra! It's your dad. Call me back."

I gently asked her a question that had been on my mind for daughters without living parents: "Do you still feel like you're doing daughtering?" Sandra told me yes, that being a daughter is an important aspect of who she is. Sandra shared how she struggled with her identity as a daughter after her parents passed away, but even though they're gone, she still feels a pride and responsibility to carry on their legacy. Sandra is just one more reminder that the daughtering role lives in the mind and heart as well as the hands and feet.

This late adulthood period in daughtering involves both reflecting on the previous life stages and continuing to cultivate legacy, tradition, and meaning for future generations. Generativity is the desire to contribute to the prosperity of younger generations in your family line, Erikson said, and is enacted both cognitively and behaviorally. As an elder daughter, you may become the keeper of family stories, the holder of traditions, as well as the guide who shares accumulated wisdom with younger family members. Even when parents are no longer present, your identity as a daughter can still flourish, rooted deeply in personal history, memory, and continuing connections.

Stillness and Rest

Some periods in life are characterized by stillness and rest, so too can your daughtering efforts. It's normal—and necessary—to pause, be still, and notice the quiet aspects of your life. You can benefit from times of rest in your relationships as much as from active nurturing. Accepting periods of relational dormancy without guilt helps ensure long-term sustainability and health in your relationships and emotional well-being.

What's "right" for each daughter can and will change over time. While you can acknowledge patterns that might relate to your life and decide to adopt behaviors or rituals similar to other women in the same life stage, you can also exercise autonomy in choosing what is right for you and your daughtering. Ultimately, accepting the fluctuations of daughterhood offers freedom from static expectations.

The Continuous Work of Lifelong Daughtering

Your daughtering journey is never finished. Being a daughter is not a task to check off a list. Daughtering evolves with you through each stage of life, asking for your attention and sometimes begging for it. There are times of intense development where you are actively investing your emotional time and care for loved ones. Other times, you can rest and take pride in a job well done.

Recognizing daughtering as continuous work is a frame of reference that appreciates that families will change. That's a good thing. New family members enter, others leave, health shifts occur, and positions are continually reassigned. You must continuously recalibrate how to mindfully engage in daughtering.

I have thought a lot about how the social construction of daughterhood means we can impact the future by training up the next generation of daughters. As my own children grow into adulthood, I feel a responsibility to share my perspective on doing family, on purpose and with intentionality. What I mean by that is I see ways to deliver my lessons about agency and authenticity to my children and I share them freely, with the goal of training them to be fantastic intergenerational relationship participants. Their daughtering and "sonning" of me will naturally shift—shaped by a changing world and evolving family dynamics. But we will approach that process mindfully.

Mindfulness must also extend to our identities and inner lives, our mental health, and well-being. As daughters, we have an obligation to ourselves to regularly check in with our emotional and relational health. It's important to remember that continuous effort at being a good daughter doesn't mean relentless exhaustion. There's a freedom in believing that powerful claim.

As you move forward, embrace daughtering as ongoing work—both joyful and challenging. Your daughtering can benefit from continual reflection, adjustment, and intentional care. This consistent practice creates a fulfilling, meaningful role that resonates deeply with your true self across your lifespan.

Predicting and Weathering the Ups and Downs

Nothing is as certain in families as difficulties, conflict, tension, and frustration. It happens because we love each other and want to be close, but also need our independence. You may not be able to prevent tension in your family, but you can anticipate it and make a strategic plan for protecting your peace from harsh outcomes. Parents and siblings can have strong reactions to new paradigms, firm boundaries, and alternative communication patterns. In short, they could get mad as hornets.

When your family gets upset about changes you want to implement, consider this: You may need to gently, yet firmly, prune unrealistic or draining expectations to foster healthier relationships. Culling the old creates space for new growth.

Recently, my friend Janelle told me, "I am ready to change, but I'm scared of how my mom and dad are going to take it. Even more, I'm worried about my sister. She's not going to like my new boundaries." And she went on to say that these hesitancies have held her back from enacting the changes that she wants, even craves. I reassured Janelle that her family is very likely to respond in just the way she said. There's no sugarcoating it. People really dislike change, especially when it's thrust upon them. But they'll live. They'll adapt and the relationship will adapt. Resistance to change often reflects fear—fear of loss, fear of discomfort, or fear that your newfound boundaries signal rejection. Anticipating these responses can help you remain steady, even in difficult conversations.

Remember Reyna, who felt exhausted managing her parents' expectations around visits with her children? While she deeply valued the time with family, the heavy weight of expectation created a burden on her energy and time. If Reyna chose to change these dynamics, she might face initial pushback or misunderstanding from her parents, who may feel confused or even hurt. But by clearly communicating her limits and perhaps suggesting alternate arrangements, Reyna could gently reshape family expectations to better reflect the reality of her life today.

And think, also, of Laney, and her clarity of choosing not to have children. Her mother's ongoing questions and subtle disappointment created emotional strain, yet Laney ultimately stood firm in her decision, patiently weathering the storm, over nearly

15 years, until her family's expectations adjusted to this new reality. She waited them out, patiently and gently.

Remember, the storms of life you experience in a family aren't inherently destructive. They can also produce positive outcomes like helping to strengthen your resolve, deepen your self-awareness, and ultimately solidify your sense of identity. Take for example the story of Yara, a 32-year-old single mom of one son. She told me how she moved to a big city to start a new career in a creative industry, leaving a steady job in her home state. Her parents' disapproval rippled through every communication, be it a phone call or visit home. Though she hoped her disappointed parents would soften over time, Yara continued to practice self-reassurance that her opinion was the one that mattered most. This was her one life and she had decided to pursue her career dream. She was not going to wait for them to agree with her before she started. These instances, though uncomfortable, become opportunities to practice compassionate assertiveness. When you think of storms in relationships as inevitable, you can maintain this perspective: The discomfort of setting new expectations won't last forever, but the benefits of healthy, authentic daughtering will endure.

Appreciating What You've Got

One last way to conceptualize your approach to daughtering is to find happiness with what already is. Sometimes the best way to approach the way to lead a good life is to step back and appreciate what we have, even if there are some thorns among the roses. This is not to say that we should stop striving for more or growing in our own skills, but there are those moments where we need to be simply still. Whether the entire family is flourishing or you are just doing the best you can, you should celebrate your accomplishments that you have cultivated in your daughtering.

Remember Vickie's newfound recognition of her own contributions? Initially, she undervalued her role. Once she recognized her role's importance, Vickie began to see her own type of daughtering as meaningful. She experienced a deeper appreciation for her distinct strengths and found pride in her indispensable contributions to her family's well-being. Vickie, too, deserved to pause, acknowledge, and enjoy the richness of the journey she had been on. She was not remaking herself into the perfect daughter, but appreciating her chosen role portrayal.

YOUR GARDEN, YOUR CHOICE

Redefining your daughterhood is a bit like gardening—only you're the gardener, and the garden is your life as a daughter. First, as any good gardener, you'd step back and see what you've got growing. You'll probably have some beautiful flowers: the parts of your daughter role that feel genuine, rewarding, and full of joy. But you'll also probably notice some weeds, too. These are the unwanted expectations, awkward conversations, and emotional drains you've been dealing with for way too long. Whether you're getting influenced by siblings, aunts, peers, or the media, you've got to know what suggestions to keep and which to dismiss. Spotting these weeds is essential because now you know exactly where to focus your attention.

Gardening is more than a fun hobby—it's down-in-the-dirt work sometimes. And daughtering can feel the same. You've got to do the tough stuff, like having those tricky conversations, setting boundaries, or tackling issues head-on. It's not always comfortable, but neither is pulling weeds on a hot day for the gardener. Yet when you finish your work, you can feel proud and hopeful because you know you've made room for better growth. Doing daughterwork is a task, but one with rewards, too.

Even when gardeners are not in their little patch of land, they are likely to still think about their garden—planning weekend work, shopping for seeds, or daydreaming about what blooms next season. Daughterthink is similar. You're always thinking ahead, planning family hangouts, or preparing mentally for tough interactions. It's all part of making sure your relationships keep thriving season after season.

Next, consider how you feel about your role. Let's face it, gardeners really love their gardens, and you can absolutely love your role as a daughter, too. It can be incredibly rewarding to see your relationships bloom, especially when you've put in the effort to nurture them. Just like gardeners get joy from butterflies and flowers, you can feel joy from the blooms of meaningful conversations, laughter, and shared moments with family. The best feelings, or daughtersentiment, we gain from daughtering keep us coming back for more.

Gardeners also proudly identify as gardeners—they join clubs, buy books, talk nonstop about gardening, and even make TikToks about it. You can totally embrace the identity work of your daughterframe in the same way. Share your stories, laugh at the craziness, and talk openly about your experiences. You never know who else might relate or even be inspired by your journey.

Every experienced gardener knows that gardens aren't static—they transform continuously, shifting through seasons of growth, dormancy, blooming, and renewal. Your daughtering is equally dynamic, evolving as you move through different stages of life. Accepting these seasonal changes can help you find peace and purpose, even in periods of transition or uncertainty. If you are in one of those seasons right now, rest assured that things can change. Whether it's a storm blowing in or a new gardener moving in next door, a lot of outside influences are unexpected and out of our control. Accepting that you and your family will change is about giving yourself permission to grow and adjust as life unfolds, just as a gardener adapts to changing weather and shifting landscapes.

Gardens are never truly "finished." They require continuous attention, adjustments, and ongoing effort. Each new season brings fresh tasks—new planting, pruning, adjusting, and careful nurturing to sustain the garden's health and beauty. A garden is a labor of love and the responsibilities to care for it never end.

The beauty of your garden doesn't come from uniformity or perfection—it arises from intentionality. Each tiny bud represents an intentional act of love, courage, or commitment you've shown. Each bloom symbolizes a boundary you've successfully maintained, a decision you've consciously made, or a meaningful connection you've nurtured.

Ultimately, doing daughtering over a lifetime comes down to two key things: tending and minding. Tending is about actively caring for your relationships—doing the real, everyday work. Minding is the thoughtful part—paying attention, being aware, and preparing for what's next. Daughtering, like a garden, can flourish and yield many fruitful blossoms.

ACTIVITY 3: EXPRESSIVE WRITING FOR UNDERSTANDING PAST DAUGHTERING

To really understand and harness your role as a daughter, it's important to examine your past and look for opportunities for growth in our future. There is a science-backed tool we can use to facilitate this evaluation, created by James Pennebaker, a social psychologist, called the Expressive Writing Paradigm. He found that when people write down their experiences, they can process their beliefs and emotions into coherent stories. You could do this in your current journal or diary, or start a new one just to track your daughtering journey.

Writing helps you take all the messy, scattered thoughts and emotions from tough experiences and turn them into a clear, organized story. This process can help you understand what happened and how you feel about it. When you write, you are creating an artifact out of your invisible thoughts. Making them tangible is an act of service to you and your inner self.

When you write about your feelings, especially difficult ones, you're giving yourself permission to release built-up stress. And each time you articulate or shape a thought into words on the page, you are taming the loose, frizzy ends of your thinking into a smoother hairstyle. In this way, you can see your past, present, and future in one space without trying to hold all the pieces together in your mind.

Finally, writing helps you reflect on the past and grow into the future. This reflection helps you see things from a new angle, and sometimes, that fresh perspective can make a bad experience feel less overwhelming. In some ways, reflecting upon your past is like watching a movie. You can be a bit distant from it or watch it from above, without being fully inside it. Only through this perspective-shifting can you move forward into a healthier future. The outcome of expressive writing can even include improved well-being, reduced stress and anxiety, and a stronger sense of self.

Try some or all these prompts to reflect on daughtering you've done in the past:

1. **Navigating Independence:** How has your relationship with your parents changed since becoming an adult? Write about the balance between seeking independence and staying connected to your family.
2. **Juggling Roles:** How do you balance the role of being a daughter with your other roles, like being a partner, a parent, or a professional? Reflect on the moments when this balance feels overwhelming and when it feels manageable.
3. **Revisiting Childhood Dynamics:** How have the dynamics from your childhood influenced your relationship with your parents today? Explore whether old roles or expectations still exist and how you are managing them.
4. **Legacy and Influence:** Reflect on the ways your parents' values, choices, or behaviors have shaped who you are today. What parts of their influence are you proud to carry forward, and what have you chosen to leave behind?

Chapter 4

DAUGHTERING OUT LOUD

IMAGINING A SOCIETY THAT SEES US

Women are giving of their time, energy, and resources to maintain healthy families, to the benefit of individuals and society. If you and I both know we're doing this work, what keeps it in the shadows? In short, patriarchy. Patriarchy is a social system that disproportionately gives power to men over women. In patriarchal social systems, men's needs and wants are considered most important and take precedence over women. This value system is observable and measurable in laws, elections, paycheck differences, and access to opportunities. Some forms of patriarchy are clear while others are less obviously observable.

Because a patriarchal social system upholds the power of men, women are often relegated to (praised and valued for) maternal and reproductive capabilities. That means, women are valued for their ability to be mothers above all else. As mothers, women contribute to a patriarchal society by providing a socially respectable outlet for sexual activity, birthing and raising children, passing on values, and molding the fabric of society. As these behaviors are reinforced, women's other potential outlets for life, family, and career, are de-emphasized.

For example, women who choose not to have children (or cannot) may find themselves diminished within a patriarchal social system, stigmatized as faulty or rebellious. On the other hand, women who choose to embrace their roles as mothers are valued and celebrated, with holidays such as Mother's Day. Our focus in this book is on daughtering, but if you're looking for a deeper dive, consider reading *Feminism Is for Everybody* by bell hooks.

The emphasis on the maternal or sexual woman doesn't leave much room for valuing a woman who is "daughterly." The narrow view of patriarchy squeezes out the many complexities of a woman's individuality and reduces her to the "maiden, mother, and crone" archetypes. Women are either sexy, mothers, or elderly.

Hey, but what about . . . ?! Yeah, yeah, we're making progress. Over the past century in the United States and around the world, women have made strides in creating equality, both in the workplace and in the home. We can vote, sign a contract without a husband, get a credit card, divorce a spouse, and go to work to break the glass ceiling. However, a woman still hasn't been elected president of the United States. Women still deal with harassment, lack of education, gender violence, and lack of access to proper medical care of their choosing. We can't get the AC the right temperature in our offices and still struggle to have a fair share of household labor done by our partners who think it's inherently feminine to unload a dishwasher. In short, we still need changes to make visible the woman's holistic, lived experience, especially on the daughtering front.

CHANGING OUR LANGUAGE: A NEW UNDERSTANDING OF FAMILY LABOR

As I indicated earlier, without the language to articulate an experience, its value remains hidden and unacknowledged. One of the fundamental steps toward social change is naming and discussing the nuances of daughtering as both a role inherent to women and also as labor, where we are using our resources to help others.

What I have noticed over the many years of introducing the word *daughtering* to people is that the term at first seems quite obvious to the listener. "Oh, yeah," they reply, "it's like when my mom helps my grandmother get her medicines from the pharmacy." And, yes, that is one form of daughtering. But a stronger and more strategic way to cement the use of the term daughtering in our lexicon is to acknowledge and proliferate the association of the term *daughtering* with the expectation of work.

The Language of Working

Work, according to organizational behavioral scholars, is broadly defined as a socially situated endeavor by people in relationships aiming to fulfill basic and higher-level needs. Basic needs include survival, while higher aspirations contribute to society, foster connection, and allow us to self-actualize. Work is an effort. Work has many more purposes beyond earning money. Working is embedded in a system of people. Working is a social connection outlet, a necessity, a vocation, and a fulfillment of our abilities.

As sociologist Naomi Gerstel describes, daughters often engage in "third shift" work, balancing career responsibilities, family care, and community involvement. This work, which extends beyond the primary career and family spheres, highlights the breadth of daughters' contributions to society. Recognizing and validating these efforts can foster a sense of belonging and worth, encouraging daughters to continue making meaningful contributions without feeling overburdened or undervalued.

Whether through traditional marketplace employment (where we earn money), family (where we keep our kin groups bonded), or community-related tasks (where we hold our real and virtual neighborhoods together), individuals are working. This is what academic types call *using our resources to pursue goals*. Working is social because it's happening within a society. And working is relational because it involves dealing with people. Looking at all aspects of working, scholars have shown that labor includes factors like emotional and power dynamics, time and intensity variations, direct and indirect efforts, and internal and external processes occurring. There's nothing simple about working. It's as complex as the people who are doing it. But these efforts come together to shape individuals and society. A deep and rich depiction of different kinds of working helps us differentiate between the forms, motivations, and impacts of labor. The more we understand the various aspects of labor and working, the more nuance we are able to see in our own forms of working.

At the heart of recognizing daughtering lies a fundamental human need: *mattering*. Counseling psychologist Donna Schultheiss identifies mattering as a psychological construct wherein individuals feel valued and their contributions recognized. For daughters, whose labor is often unacknowledged, the absence of recognition can be deeply disheartening. Acknowledging daughtering reaffirms the value of these roles, underscoring that their contributions to family and community are both meaningful and essential.

Daughtering's Economic Valuation

Doing daughtering involves small, everyday actions that are easy to overlook or ignore. These tiny actions might seem unimportant to those who would dismiss a daughter's work as something inherent or expected, but these building blocks are what build family relationships and keep generations close.

Doing this kind of work depletes your resources; you only have so much time and energy in a day. When you spend those limited commodities on daughtering, then you have less available for other important parts of your life, like your career, raising your kids, friendships, community activities, and especially your self-care. There's only so much you can give before you burn out. So, when we give our daughterwork to our families, the least we deserve is for it to be appreciated, valued, and treasured.

How do we assess the ways daughtering benefits a family? Perhaps we calculate the monetary hourly wage a daughter might make. Many management and labor scholars study the use of resources and company time. Theoretically, an activity that takes up resources can be monetarily assessed. In this sense, we could create an hourly cost of doing daughtering and calculate an annual salary for women doing this work within families (and of course the cost of missed career, leisure, or sleeping time while doing daughtering).

There are two ways to do this. The first is to account for the wage the woman is currently making in her career, and evaluate how much she would be paid at the same rate to do daughtering. For example, let's say a woman typically makes $25 an hour while at her daily job. If she diverts a half hour of her time to take a call from her mom who is frustrated with a family member and "talks her down off the ledge," then she has used $12.50 worth of time daughtering. (Let's put aside whether she stays late at her job to make up for this cost taken during the workday.) If a daughter provides a few hours a week in daughtering, by being on the phone or visiting, spending her time thinking about the future or making firm plans, she's diverted about $60 of her weekly resources toward daughtering. But, of course, nobody will be paying her. These are estimates of her time value.

Another way to calculate daughtering is to determine the market rate of the task if another person was hired to do it. For example, if a therapist was hired to listen to Mom for half an hour, that might cost $50 (at a $100/hourly rate for professional counseling). The value, then, of a daughter listening to her mother as her sounding board for multiple hours in a month might be $500 of her time spent in emotional labor for her family.

On the one hand, it's validating to consider creating a numeric valuation like this one. It's like going on the entrepreneurial investment television show *Shark Tank* and having the investors affirm what your leadership and vision are worth, even before there are sales or customers. Gauging the worth of unpaid work, particularly women's care work, highlights its societal importance, underscoring the role of care in social significance.

However, a purely economic view may be misleading, implying that all unpaid work can be substituted. You may find yourself saying, "Yeah, but what if the daughter *likes* talking to her mom and being a listening ear for her?" Economic reasoning alone cannot fully capture the personal benefit and satisfaction of performing certain care tasks oneself. It's an imperfect system to imagine the costs of doing daughtering strictly from a monetary standpoint. Not everyone *wants* to hire someone else to do the daughtering for them. It's not precisely right to place a dollar amount on our hourly output of daughtering, maybe even a bit icky. In many ways, we *want* to do daughtering.

And sometimes we do daughtering while doing other things, too. I could be on the phone with my mom while also folding laundry or watching my kids play in the pool. So, somebody might argue, I'm not exclusively doing daughtering during that time and therefore couldn't count up the cost of an hourly wage. But, I would argue back, just imagine a childcare worker in a daycare environment. They might actually *like* watching children and also be good at it. They might get personal satisfaction and fulfillment doing their job well. They might even make a grocery list on their phone while watching kids on the playground (while getting paid). So, the truth is that all kinds of work overlap, and creating economic valuations is difficult. It's probably best left to the economists.

And that's where we come back to how economists have shown, over the past several years, how economic rates for women's work can give us insight into social and domestic issues. Oxfam, a global organization dedicated to ending poverty and injustice, estimates women and girls around the world perform approximately 10 *trillion* US dollars' worth in unpaid labor. *Annually.*

Oxfam says women and girls are the "hidden engine" that keeps economies, businesses, and societies turning. And that labor comes at a cost. Many of these women lack access to education and are kept from the labor force, which denies them opportunities and continues a cycle of poverty.

These struggles highlight the problem of hidden labor but can also be distracting for those of us who think, "Well, I'm not getting water for my village, so this doesn't apply to me." Much of the discourse surrounding family care at the government and policy level focuses on caregiving for the aging population or care in lower-income countries. And these conversations are both important and necessary.

But now, we must take that same argument and apply it to the hidden labor in our lives. For many of you reading this book, that's the everyday labor of daughtering that is eating away at your resources and chipping away parts of your identity as your labor goes unnoticed and underappreciated. Without knowing it, you might also be losing career opportunities, have diminished health and well-being, and be risking burnout—all because society cannot see the impact of all you are providing.

More than an understanding of illness or childcare, my argument is that we must also take a look at the everyday care experiences in families throughout the middle portion of life, where women are binding families together through nominal, yet multitudinal acts of support that build the everyday family experience.

Discussing these labors is important to naming an experience, and language has the capacity to shape both thought and behavior, impacting how society values certain roles. Language expert Muriel Schulz said, "A rich vocabulary on a given subject reveals an area of concern of the society whose language is being studied." When language is nestled in a patriarchal system, according to Schulz, words will favor men and derogate women. Terms for women most likely to escape this trap are those related to mothering and motherhood. The fact that we don't have words to describe what daughters do is how we know that society cares very little for its impact. That does not correlate, however, with a lack of necessity for daughtering.

Language and the Patriarchy

The power of naming daughtering connects to something called "muted group theory," which suggests that marginalized groups struggle to voice their experiences because dominant discourse fails to reflect them. Coined by anthropologists Edwin and Shirley Ardener, this theory explains how societal structures privilege certain narratives while suppressing others. Daughtering, unlike motherhood, lacks the prominence and vocabulary to fully occupy public discourse.

Without dedicated terms and discussions, the labor of daughters slips into the shadows of family life, obscured by broader cultural narratives that privilege the mother-child relationship. Daughters must therefore adapt, fitting their experiences into a societal mold that fails to capture the breadth of their work.

But we can begin to create the changes we want to see in society by using terminology around our relationships effectively. First, we must resist the urge to equate daughterhood with womanhood, and womanhood with motherhood. To fully understand daughtering, we need a language that clarifies the contributions daughters make and the unique challenges they face.

We can be part of the change to our vernacular by using terminology that applies to daughtering—and avoiding the words that don't work. This is our *discursive power*. Discursive power refers to our ability to use knowledge, discussion, and cultural "talk" to frame ideas and influence social thought.

The writing of this book is an act of discursive power. When you link arms with me, using the language appropriate to our new understanding of daughtering and daughterhood, we collaboratively influence our social world. By noticing which discourses are prominent (mothers) and which are absent (daughters) from our social world, we can first see the issue and then make a change.

I remember when I first shared my ideas about the language of daughtering with my mom; from that day forward, she started telling me, "Thanks for daughtering me today." It may seem so small or even silly to hear your mom compliment you for a job well done, but I find that it hits the spot. I did some daughtering, she noticed and praised me, and because I feel valued, I am renewed to do more good daughtering another day.

Changing the System: Policy and Structural Shifts

To truly recognize the value of daughtering in families and society, we have to also transform the structures in our society that hold us back—from economic policies and workplace practices to social expectations. Currently, many traditional family policies acknowledge only caregiving roles with minor children, elder parents, or supporting individuals with significant health needs. These policies overlook daughtering responsibilities. Daughters needing time off work for family-related responsibilities may have to rely on their own paid time off (PTO) or face financial losses. This happened recently to my friend Kerri who is a single, child-free woman in her late 30s. She recently took off work to help her dad after a knee-replacement surgery. She told me that there was some chatter at work about why she wasn't around and it seemed like her colleagues thought it was not a valid reason to be gone. To them, having a sick kid at home would be a reasonable excuse, but doing daughtering wasn't. This kind of workplace loss and reputational damage is hard to quantify, but no less important to consider.

Rarely are there specific policies addressing the needs and contributions of daughters. It's left up to each organization to create a policy or implement a plan. When that doesn't happen, daughters have to find their own way forward, often at the price of personal sacrifice. This limited approach prevents society from fully recognizing the substantial and distinctive support daughters offer to their families. To address these structural inequalities, we need more comprehensive policies and legal frameworks that explicitly acknowledge, value, and support the essential family labor provided by daughters.

Policies and Patriarchy

Patriarchal systems also influence family policy and labor laws, which traditionally prioritize mothers' responsibilities over daughters' roles. This narrow framing limits opportunities for daughters to receive societal support, effectively rendering their contributions invisible. Instead of supporting daughters who provide valuable family care, these policies indirectly pressure women to prioritize mothering, creating an environment where daughtering is devalued.

If your workplace offered a leave-policy related to parenting obligations, would you take it? Yes . . . if you're a parent. But many women are not parents. New-to-the-workforce twentysomethings are often not yet parents. Fifty-year-olds may no longer be parents of minor children. To be clear, no one is suggesting that parental-leave policies are unfair or unnecessary. Rather, this is a discussion of what *more* our structural systems could do to support those who are doing the social reproductive labor that moves our society forward. And that means supporting women with practical policies.

Policy Reform

For genuine progress, we need systemic change that includes policies acknowledging all forms of family care, including daughtering. Integrating daughtering into the Family and Medical Leave Act (FMLA) could create pathways for adult daughters to take time off work without the fear of job loss. Expanding family leave policies to explicitly recognize care for parents, siblings, and other family members would better reflect the range of familial duties daughters perform. Flexible work options and better caregiver support programs could empower daughters and relieve some of their burdens.

What if workplaces offered time off work for daughtering? Women could meet some of their obligations without stigma, expanding the narrative of women's work beyond motherhood. Current systems prioritize maternal leave but overlook the invisible labor adult daughters contribute—creating inequities and undervaluing essential care work. As daughters become acknowledged in policies, even in the smallest of ways, the work of women becomes more visible.

Including nonmarket labor in economic indicators like GDP would also elevate the essential role of unpaid care. Countries like New Zealand and Canada are already experimenting with these models. By rethinking economic indicators, especially in the world's most developed countries, societies can highlight the indispensable role of social reproductive labor in sustaining family and community structures.

While measuring care work's economic value can be challenging, approaches like time-use surveys provide estimates for the hours spent in family care, which can then be translated into an equivalent financial value. The American Time Use Survey (ATUS, https://www.bls.gov/tus/) measures how people spend time doing activities like paid work, childcare, volunteering, and socializing, but it falls short. Surveys like these exclude the microcare activities like emotional support and multitasking, and anything that an adult child does for their parent who is under 65. Especially important is when daughters are "watching over" their parents, or *metadaughtering*; daughters are doing the executive-level work of the coordinating and supervising family bonding. With outdated and limited study designs like self-reporting using time-use diaries, a lot of daughtering falls through the cracks. It's not recognized in the data, so it doesn't get translated into policy.

Shifting Expectations

Over the past century, expectations for women have evolved significantly. The women's movement brought about increased access to education, career opportunities, and autonomy, challenging traditional gender roles that confined women to the home. However, despite these advances, women today still often face persistent expectations to provide emotional and logistical support for family members.

For many daughters, balancing career and family is made more challenging by the segmentation of family roles under capitalism. Capitalistic social views have taught Western women, in particular, to think of most everything through the lens of transaction. Even relationships can be thought of as transactional. And you might not even know you're doing it. This perspective implies that daughters "owe" their families support, creating an unspoken expectation of availability. To combat this, daughters must intentionally craft the boundaries and balance that respects their personal needs while fulfilling their family roles.

Let's go over a few practical strategies for balancing the demands of career and family life, with a particular focus on intentionality and resilience. You can be empowered to take control of your life and make changes by cleaning up your own house (metaphorically, of course).

With Parents: Openly communicate your availability and boundaries. Digital tools like shared calendars can help synchronize family care responsibilities. My sister shares her family calendar with everyone in the household, but also with both sets of grandparents. They know they are invited to join in activities that are labeled as shared events in the app, but it's their responsibility to check it. Establishing physical and mental boundaries prevents burnout, ensuring that your contributions remain sustainable. Another strategy to manage daughtering responsibilities with parents is to make "invisible" time visible. Don't hesitate to "narrate" your daughtering. The goal is not to make others feel indebted to us, but rather to have our work become noticeable. Showing what we *are doing* can also clarify why we're not available for *other* events or tasks. Even if you choose not to share it, you can track your own time doing daughtering so you have a full accounting of your labors. It's like the time-use diary we wish we could see from all daughters.

With the Workplace: Make use of family leave policies and other benefits that support work-life balance. Advocating for workplace flexibility not only benefits you but also normalizes the idea of supporting family care responsibilities. When our colleagues know we are using the inclusive workplace opportunities, they can support us and keep the policies on the books. The rise of the gig economy (where workers subsist on multiple jobs rather than one main career) may eventually grant more individuals autonomy over their time, but daughters must advocate for these rights in traditional work environments as well.

Over the past few years in my workplace, I've seen how one employee has normalized her daughtering to the whole group. Like the time she sent an email to the entire department saying, "My dad needs my help with the horses today, so I'll be in about two hours late." It both lets us know where she is and why she's not reachable for a bit, but also normalizes the everyday daughtering activities we do for our parents, making them both seem reasonable to work on and acceptable to take time away from the workplace to manage.

With Siblings: Engage siblings in family care discussions, emphasizing the shared responsibility of supporting parents. Daughters (especially the eldest and sometimes the geographically closest) can feel pressure to shoulder the majority of care work. Collective family involvement can distribute the responsibilities, fostering a healthier balance for everyone involved. If resistance arises, daughters can take a "shift and persist" approach—continuing to propose ways siblings can contribute while adapting to feedback. Don't give up just because your sister gets a little salty with you. Shift to another strategic approach and persist in your efforts to collaboratively tackle family responsibilities.

One daughter I spoke with told me that she couldn't get her brother to help with any kind of conflict or relationship dynamics in the family, year after year. So instead, one day she asked him to go on a drive with the dads and uncles during the family holiday. He ended up taking all the men of the family for a quick round of golf and some milkshakes before coming back to the house. Later he told her that all the guys got to blow off steam, talk a bit, and laugh. It was, in the end, a helper for "relationship dynamics" in the family without him even knowing that he was doing it. She had found a win-win way to get her brother involved.

Even when family members are initially resistant to change, they may gradually become more open to shared responsibilities as they see the value of a balanced caregiving dynamic. Remember that every family member contributes in unique ways. Acknowledge the care you see others doing and they'll likely be more amenable to recognizing your care or even doing more on their end.

Taking Control of Your Daughtering Role

While societal structures may limit the support available for daughtering, individual daughters can take steps to balance their lives within these constraints. The work of daughtering is complex, but we don't have to accept the status quo. We can work to make impactful changes for a better, brighter future of daughtering in the world. By establishing boundaries and advocating for systemic changes, daughters can change their lives—and by extension, inspire broader changes in how society values their contributions. Daughters can take control of our futures by having a vision.

ACTIVITY 4: ROADMAP TO A BETTER DAUGHTERING EXPERIENCE

Create a visual "road map" to notice your daughtering and set out for an improved destination. You can do this individually or with your family members.

Materials Needed
- Large paper or whiteboard
- Markers or pens
- Sticky notes
- Timer

Instructions:
1. **Draw a long and windy road.** Begin by drawing a road across the entire space of the whiteboard or large paper. This road symbolizes your path of daughtering so far. The events on this road are instances from the past that have been meaningful in your life's journey.
2. **Define daughtering.** At the top of your blank space, above the road you just drew, write out your own definition of what "daughtering" means to you (or anyone participating). This ensures a consistent (and shared!) understanding of the concept.
3. **Place your signs.** Draw some road signs along the way that signify milestones in your daughtering journey. Milestones in your life might be big events like a graduation, marriage, moving to a new state or country, having a child, death

of a loved one, or even a big argument. For each of these significant milestones in your life, write a short description of the key event and why it was significant.

4. **Identify the "YAY."** Take five minutes to identify some things that made you go "YAY!" as a daughter in your adult life up to now. These "yay" moments could be times you set a boundary, felt loved, resolved a conflict, or made a big decision. Write these *positive* daughtering experiences on sticky notes. Stick these notes on the board or paper, near the milestones, creating a collage of positive attributes. The goal is to identify how an event had a positive or negative emotional impact.

5. **Identify the "YUCK."** Using a different color pen or paper, take five minutes to identify daughtering experiences that made you feel "YUCK!" Write these down (with vigor!) and stick them on the paper or board near where they occurred on the timeline or road map. You may notice that an event has both a Yay and Yuck sticky note. That's okay; two things can be true.

6. **Ponder.** View your board for two minutes. Take it in. Observe how the YAY and YUCK may have occurred simultaneously. Or perhaps there was a long period of one or the other. Or maybe the YAY stopped and hasn't restarted. Observe, breathe, feel feelings, and find insights that help you understand the journey you've been on so far.

7. **Place signs for the future.** Draw a few road signs going into the future. These signify events you look forward to happening.

8. **Develop actionable steps.** Think of some action steps you can take with these future events in mind. What can you do to get there? What can you do to enhance your daughtering experience *now*? What can you learn about your past experiences that will inform your future?

Chapter 5

INTERSECTIONAL PERSPECTIVES ON DAUGHTERING

When doing studies, researchers can start by making a positionality statement, which is a way to share how the researcher's background shapes what they see and report on. Since most of my research is qualitative—that is, gathered with the goal of an in-depth understanding of human perspectives and behavior—my positionality statement reveals how my own lived experiences are part of data interpretation. Writing this kind of statement about myself is for transparency, which is especially important for this chapter on intersectional identities.

I'm a married white woman with two teenage children. I was raised and still live in the southwestern United States by married parents who are still together. I was educated in public schools all the way through my doctorate and now I teach at a private Christian university. My focus on families, communication, gender, and labor comes from a feminist lens—meaning, I see women as equal and worthy of fair treatment. I think daughtering and care in families is undervalued and invisible, so I spend much of my efforts trying to call attention to this divide.

I realize that elements of my social identity create a privileged worldview. But as a trained social scientist, I actively try to stay reflective and open to learning from the women I interview and write about. In this work, I hear about a lot of situations and stories that are dissimilar to my own, and I include them because it's most important to me to demonstrate that all daughtering matters and can help us understand the bigger picture of the world we live in. The best parts of my job are finding out something new that was previously hidden, misunderstood, and is now recovered.

I invite you to read this chapter as the beginning of a conversation starter—and not the full and final word on any topic. There's much more to say and many voices that deserve to be heard. In these pages, you'll read about histories, resistance, and community; these are pillars that help us deepen our understanding of what it means to do daughtering for all kinds of people.

GENDER AND SEXUALITY FOR DAUGHTERS

Daughtering is shaped by gender, sexuality, and the dynamics of female subjectivity—or the ability of women to speak knowingly of their own experiences. And daughters develop a sense of self through relationships, emotional labor, and mutual recognition—especially with their moms. Gender plays a significant role in this journey, as gendered experiences can reinforce traditional norms for daughters. Female subjectivity, like gender itself, is fluid and evolving—shaped by cultural context, personal relationships, and the ongoing negotiation of identity.

I'll share with you the story of my friend Jordan. For the first 25 years of his life, he lived his life as a female. In his 20s, he realized he wanted to live his life as a man. As you can imagine, he and I have had some fascinating conversations about what it's like to live as a man who was raised to be a daughter.

Specifically, Jordan has shared that while he was raised to do daughtering by considering everyone's feelings and being attentive in communication and caring, he's noticed that most men don't even think about these types of behaviors. Jordan spent years watching other men to determine how to assimilate his mannerisms and movements, learning where and how men stand during family gatherings, and examining how men communicate with one another. He did these things to "unlearn" the feminine behaviors he was molded toward in childhood, adolescence, and emerging adulthood as a woman.

He had to learn to shed the intense concerns and questioning women do to "help" in a gathering, instead standing back along the sides of the room and waiting for someone else to get the event started and clean up. He told me that he noticed "worry" and "daughtering" had gone hand in hand for him, so letting go of the pressures of daughtering released him from a lot of stress. Now, Jordan has the benefit of having other siblings in his family, including brothers and sisters. He can release his daughtering responsibilities without feeling like he has abandoned his parents. And he can view a close-up version of "sonning" the way his family members do it.

Without a doubt, the considerations of daughtering in a family when you've transitioned are complicated. I only have Jordan's perspective, but it is apparent to me that his entire family is adjusting in different ways. Yes, over 15 years later, they still seem to be figuring it out. And that has to do with their feelings about gender, sexuality, religion, culture, politics, and more. Families with individuals who have fluid or changing gender identities can expect to navigate complex and challenging thoughts and conversations. For some individuals, this starts as simply as changing their pronouns from she/her to they/them. For others, like Jordan, it's more definitively transitioning to he/him language.

Beyond gender identity, there are the ways in which sexuality can complicate daughtering. While some Freudian scholars believe the father to be the object from which girls draw to understand their sexuality, some scholars say it's actually the mother who is the epicenter of initial sexual revelation. Young children identify with their mother's body first and then perhaps later begin to disidentify with it.

And, of course, mothers are the point of reference of many social messages for daughters, setting the family's standards for acceptable femininity, especially around dating, marriage, and reproduction. Daughters are particularly influenced by mothers in their own body image. Author and therapist Hillary L. McBride says the way women speak about their bodies can significantly influence daughters' self-image. Daughters can inherit detrimental beliefs about their bodies, even subtle ones. But McBride says the way to combat negative body image, which is your idea of the body's appearance, is through embodiment, which is the lived life of the body. In short, a mother who enjoys her body shows a daughter that it's possible to enjoy her body as well. And while it doesn't help anyone to assign blame, it is important to recognize your caregivers as a key site for intergenerational transmission of cultural, gender, and sexuality ideas. Excitingly, you can have a role in changing these attitudes for the next generation.

As we continue to embrace the variability in doing daughtering, an important step is noticing the intersectionality and diversity of the women inhabiting the daughter role. This is the first step, according to noted feminist writer Kimberlé Crenshaw, in recognizing how gender, race, class, and sexuality shape expectations of individuals at the intersection of these identities in complex ways.

Applying a lens of intersectionality can help us challenge existing notions of what it means to do daughtering by looking at more than the process of the role portrayal, but also noticing the systems that can hinder some individuals from doing it well. Only by dismantling racial and class-based hierarchies, or noticing who is unsupported in their attempts to daughter others, can we begin to confront the realities of daughtering today.

Even more than 30 years ago, Janneke van Mens-Verhulst, Karlein Schreurs, and Liesbeth Woertman, the authors of *Daughtering and Mothering: Female Subjectivity Reanalysed*, were calling for a new way of thinking about daughtering. It's unhelpful when we center the experiences of daughters from a white, Northern European, and Anglo-American point of view, because we only get a partial picture. The following sections will further explore the goal of thinking about daughtering in new ways, or in ways that have been expressed but ignored in past research.

OPPRESSIVE AND OPPRESSED DAUGHTERHOOD (AND MOTHERHOOD)

Up to this point, daughtering has been described as a role, a shared community, and a hidden labor. This chapter is about pointing out all the ways daughterhood can be conceived, and for some, that is as a site of oppression.

Poet and social justice pioneer Adrienne Rich critiqued the roles women play as being shaped by patriarchal systems. Patriarchy is not just in our laws and policies but also shows up in family life. Strict gender roles, she said in her late 1970s writings, limit women in families and reduce their ability to make changes on an individual level. Mothers, shaped by their rigid roles, impact daughters. Patriarchal mothering creates unspoken tensions and limitations, which continues a repeating cycle of inequality. Even though moms want to elevate their daughters and help them have great lives, restrictive systems limit what they can achieve. Still, they share an intensity in their bond that conveys a mother's willingness to give her daughter the world.

Later in the 1980s, humanities professor and activist Bettina Aptheker, author of *Tapestries of Life: Women's Work, Women's Consciousness, and the Meaning of Daily Experience*, wrote about tackling the overwhelming and oppressive big systems of control through small, everyday instances. Her work reminds us that even routine activities can make inroads against difficult conditions. For daughters, this means first noticing gendered expectations and then taking actions in even the smallest ways.

Here's something I did a couple years ago: I stopped buying

my mother-in-law's gifts. I still discuss her gifts with my husband, but she's his mom and it's up to him to purchase something for her. This past year, he came up with a flower bouquet delivery every month for the upcoming year. She loved it more than any single gift I had come up with in the past ten years. So, it was a win-win-win for her, for my husband, and for me.

On this topic, history and women's studies professor Elsa Barkley Brown, author of the article "Mothers of Mind," added another layer of insight. She said that motherhood and reciprocal actions of daughtering can also be a site for empowerment. She emphasized that women are not just holders of their mothers' stories but also can participate in shaping them. Daughtering becomes a space for negotiation, where dignity and resistance can flourish. As I think about the future when my own son and daughter are adults, I look forward to seeing them exert their own influence—or agency— within our families, because I treasure their unique qualities and am curious to see where our family goes and what we will become. I have never wanted to be surrounded by good little soldiers, but instead to have smart people around whose company I enjoy and by whom I am willing to be shaped. Brown called this "transforming histories into futures." Daughtering is active and dynamic. It can also be a communal, ancestral, and shared experience.

OTHERMOTHERING, THE MOTHERLINE, AND COMMUNAL DAUGHTERING

Some daughters are cared for by relatives like aunts and grandparents who step in when there's a need. This practice is related to the idea of *othermothering*, a tradition originating in West Africa and found throughout the African diaspora involving women caring for children who are not their own, both formally and informally, as an arrangement of communal rearing. When women are pressed into communal mothering, they can undergo complex identity shifts as they begin to think of themselves in a new maternal way.

Daughters can also be othermothered, on the receiving end of care. Author and activist Patricia Hill Collins has written extensively of othermothering and the responsibility of women in communities to be motherly and daughterly to one another. The tasks, though often related to supporting minor children in the wider community, which also supports the kids' biological mother, can be extended to adult daughter support as well.

I first learned about daughtering as a Black feminist ideology and epistemological worldview when I interviewed mother-daughter duo Leah and Mildred Boveda for a podcast episode. Leah began by sharing her experience as a youth activist in the Critical Race Theory debates. She experienced challenges getting her voice heard but found some adults who ultimately supported her. The Bovedas use the lens of daughtering in a published research article to share the story of how Leah daughtered the nonfamilial adults in her life. They tied this experience to the lens of Black feminism and communal daughtering, describing how throughout her journey of daughtering, Leah was both pushing and appreciating the othermothers in her life.

Daughtering, the Bovedas described, can also be viewed as a form of activism. Scholar Venus Evans-Winters has said that the concept of daughtering is used to explore the experience of Black girls and women who have been raised in a culture of othermothering. Daughtering, according to Evans-Winters, is a shared act among women who live out their inherited responsibility to witness their culture, retain secrets, or share stories from elders. Though there is limited academic scholarship on this form of communal daughtering, Mildred Boveda advocates for us to remember that theorizing on mothering and daughtering matters, even when its evidence is not seen in formal journal publications. Boveda notes that her own beloved mother had little access to formal education but conveyed many daughtering lessons.

I was grateful to listen to and learn from the Bovedas about the ways institutional systems and policies can mute or marginalize ideas from some communities while simultaneously amplifying majority voices. Daughtering is everywhere. Mothering and other forms of women's role labors are happening whether we acknowledge it or not. Importantly, the Bovedas urged me to consider the idea of how power differences impact what we notice and pay attention to.

Leah told me that if you are considering the roles of mother and daughter and conceptualizing one or the other as being more powerful or in control, then you're missing the mark. Instead, she said to consider mothering and daughtering as two people with a united goal. These roles are two sides of the same coin. Daughters are not dismissed, diminished, or devalued in their role. Mothers are not superior, always right, and all-knowing. Rather, there's communication, love, and respect between them.

Functionally, the practice of mothering and daughtering in the Black community is continually evolving and changing, but the goal remains consistent, and that is to create community. Daughtering, as a response to othermothering, can be conceptualized as a process of relationality, mutuality, respect, and influence.

Novelist Toni Morrison recast mothering among Black Americans as a communal public act of survival. She helped readers reimagine mothering as a collective and ancestral responsibility, tapping into our duty for generativity—preparing the next generation for what's to come. Where Anglo or white mothering is often perceived as an individual and personal act, Black mothering is inherently tied to community preservation.

Through the motherline—that is, a woman's lineage through her mother and female ancestors—daughters inherit stories, wisdom, and the "being" part of daughtering—their identity within a family and a collective. Listening to stories is a central act of daughtering, according to Evans-Winters, as it taps into a heightened awareness and historical consciousness that deepens our connection to one another. It is an opportunity for flourishing to connect so deeply with the women from our past who guide us forward.

Don't overlook these stories as simple "women's talk," says poet and activist Naomi Ruth Lowinsky. Each narrative we lose is like losing a part of ourselves and our history in the motherline. These bits of "female lore" Lowinsky says, are powerful tools for healing and cultural continuity.

DAUGHTERING AS ACTIVISM

Have you ever before thought of using your daughter role as a tool for change?

Daughtering becomes a form of activism when you move beyond your personal experiences and think of the larger social systems. With intentional actions, daughtering can become a catalyst.

Daughtering as activism allows us to accept what those before us have done (or not done), and move beyond it through forgiveness and onto change and even cultural reshaping.

Merle Woo, a Chinese American feminist writer, says that activism is an extension of personal experience, when you see your struggles as connected to larger systems of oppression. Whether it be capitalism, imperialism, heteronormativity, or patriarchal ideals, the systems you live in are influential to your moment-to-moment existence. They're not nothing; nor are they escapable or unrelated to the daughtering you are doing in your own home. Instead, Woo says, liberation comes from an awareness of the oppression we live under, but even more pertinently, those our parents have lived under and failed to escape.

Rather than blaming our parent for failing to provide something more you needed, we can thank our parents for their sacrifice and see how their struggles made a way for us to do more in our lifetime. Woo writes: "[D]o you realize, Ma, that I could never have reacted the way I have if you had not provided for me the opportunity to be free of the binds that have held you down, and to be in the process of self-affirmation?" After embracing the generational sacrifices, the next step is to extend our parents' work to change the systems we live under and within.

You can engage in activism by storytelling, political engagement, or even by making and holding space in your own sphere of influence. But, most important, Woo says the first step toward transformative activism is to embrace your own humanity by loving yourself. This also means sharing your stories. Woo writes to her mother as a form of forgiveness, which is also a form of activism: "Because of your life, because of . . . all those gifts you never received, I saw myself as having worth; now I begin to love myself more, see our potential, and fight for just that kind of social change that will affirm me, my race, my sex, my heritage. While I affirm myself, Ma, I affirm you." Transforming our views on daughtering means embracing the ways we are worthy as we do it and loving the act of daughtering and the privilege to be in this role.

DAUGHTERING AS RADICAL LOVE

Radical love is not about loving your parent with hugs or affection, but loving them with a knowing that notices their trials, forgives their inadequacies, and embraces the privileges they have provided you. That's the essence of an argument made by Cherríe Moraga, an American Chicana writer and activist: to keep love as your key emotion when thinking of how to change the world.

She says that love is more than just an emotion but an action. She views love—both for your parent and for your community—as a radical force that fuels resistance and sustains marginalized communities. Moraga's concept of active love insists that you do not passively inherit the past but take responsibility for how you carry it forward, choosing to love in a way that liberates rather than confines. Her writing suggests that when love is rooted in truth-telling, vulnerability, and a commitment to justice, it becomes a force capable of dismantling oppressive systems.

Particularly for women whose family stories have been erased, like those of immigrant families, love can be a tool to resist a deep depression and sadness for all that has been lost. We can also build our daughterhood community with other women by embracing our joy in doing daughtering, even with its struggles. Solidarity can be built through loving engagement.

In an interview with *People* magazine, actor Uzo Aduba, an American raised by Nigerian parents, shared the grief and pain of carrying, birthing, and raising her first child after her mother died from cancer. She weaves her personal stories with interviews from family members in a book about being raised by a strong matriarch and becoming a powerful daughter. She shared in the interview that even though her mother died, she continues to feel her presence living inside her, as part of her identity as a daughter. "I'm wildly surprised with every day how much of [my mom] Nonyem lives literally inside of me," Aduba says. "How some of the things that she said to me, my sibling growing up come out of me. My mom is famous for going, 'No, no, no,' when she talking to you. The first time it came out of my mouth, I was like, 'Who said that?' I promise you, I never said this before."

Aduba's storytelling shows the gifts that can come from the motherline; these are often experiences that delight our souls and bring us comfort as we connect from a daughter's perspective to our mother's past.

Bringing It Back to What We Share

Care and the invisible labor associated with it looks different around the globe, but daughters are a key feature in care systems and the maintenance of family. What unites us is the emotional weight we carry, as we juggle both tradition and the pressures of modern life. Regardless of the culture, daughters find themselves at the intersection of family expectations and their own personal aspirations. Whether through hands-on care, emotional support, or balancing family traditions with modern life, the core challenge of daughters to carry an invisible emotional and mental load for our families remains the same.

Daughters all over the world face similar pressures and challenges, but in diverse contexts and settings. The lessons from different cultural groups and ideologies can be used to inform our own lives and future decision-making as we mindfully decide how we want to exist in the world as daughters. With open eyes to diverse daughtering strategies, daughters can begin to navigate family duties by flexing our autonomy of choice. And that choice might just include traditional rituals and maintenance of kinship routines from bygones past. Or you can make the choice of the daughter who will forge a new path and leave behind the tug of duty and obligation to ancestors she never met. Both are beautiful choices.

UNIVERSAL ROLE, UNIQUE EXPRESSIONS

Families—those intricate webs of connections—are like snowflakes. No two are exactly alike. But those snowflakes do clump together to make predictable patterns. And that's true of daughtering around the world. No matter where you're reading this from around the world, we likely share some daughtering while embracing your own cultural traditions. Yet despite cultural differences, daughtering remains a central part of family life across the globe. However, the ways in which daughters contribute to their families vary widely.

GLOBE DIMENSIONS

People often have different expectations and conversations about daughterhood, depending on their cultural backgrounds. Culture can mean a lot of things, but generally, it includes the attitudes, beliefs, values, and habits that groups of people share. Anthropologists and social psychologists have spent a lot of time studying how different cultural perspectives shape the way people think and communicate.

The GLOBE (Global Leadership and Organizational Behavior Effectiveness) project provides a few ways to think about cultural similarities and differences. This typology includes nine cultural dimensions that describe how societies define their values and practices. The dimensions are: power distance (how a community accepts authority power distribution), uncertainty avoidance (describes discomfort with ambiguity and preference for rules), institutional collectivism (emphasizes collective action and sharing resources), in-group collectivism (highlights loyalty and pride with close others), gender egalitarianism (assesses how gender differences are minimized or amplified), assertiveness (measures how competitive and confrontational people act), future orientation (describes the focus on planning and investing), performance orientation (assesses how achievement is valued), and humane orientation (describes sentiment toward fairness and kindness). These cultural factors can really shape how we see daughterhood enacted around the world—and how we gauge just about everything else. Below are several examples of how these dimensions can offer a framework for daughtering.

Conceptualizing Daughtering Around the World Through Metaphor

What I have learned in my years of describing daughtering is that women around the world come to this framework differently. Cultural dimensions are not just abstract ideas—they deeply shape how people across the world think about family roles, especially daughterhood. The metaphors below provide insight into how women in different cultures might conceptualize their role as daughters, revealing rich and nuanced understandings of identity, obligation, and love.

While my tendency as an American is to think of the economic costs and benefits of doing daughtering, others frame the role quite differently. Below are a few metaphors of daughtering that might resonate with you.

A Tree with Deep Roots and Spreading Branches

Cultural dimensions: in-group collectivism (family loyalty and ties), future orientation (investment in long-term familial success), and gender egalitarianism (freedom to grow independently).

This metaphor represents adult daughters as independent individuals who grow outward into their own identities, while still maintaining meaningful connections to their familial origins. The individualism dimension emphasizes personal growth and autonomy, allowing daughters to spread their branches freely. Simultaneously, the long-term orientation highlights the importance placed on maintaining a firm family base, while exercising personal independence to build a bright future. Daughters who share this type of story are expected to grow independently (spreading branches) while maintaining strong connections and support for their families (deep roots).

A Bridge Between Generations

Cultural dimensions: in-group collectivism (connection across generations), future orientation (preserving culture and family over time), and power distance (respecting traditional family hierarchies).

Adult daughters can serve as a connector for families wanting to link their storied past with the modern challenges of the present and an eye on a bright future ahead. The bridge symbolizes the daughters' crucial role in preserving cultural and family traditions (long-term orientation) and maintaining harmonious relationships (collectivism). High-power distance, or comfort with distinct power structures (think military-style leadership), acknowledges the clear, respected positions within the family structure that daughters are shaped by over a lifetime.

Adult daughters play a crucial role in connecting and supporting both their parents and future generations, maintaining traditions and family unity.

A Lotus Blooming in a Pond

Cultural dimensions: gender egalitarianism (balancing femininity with autonomy), in-group collectivism (anchoring in family), and power distance (operating within structured family roles).

This metaphor represents adult daughters skillfully balancing personal aspirations with societal and family expectations. A blossoming lotus flower represents the cultural value of femininity, which is focused on quality of life and enjoyment of beauty. Collectivism emphasizes the importance of family relationships, while high-power distance signals clearly defined family roles and obligations. The lotus, thriving in its environment while remaining deeply connected to its roots, symbolizes the balance between personal growth and family obligations.

A Pillar of Strength in the Family Home

Cultural dimensions: in-group collectivism (supporting family unity), power distance (respect for structure and defined roles), uncertainty avoidance (valuing stability), short-term orientation (focus on obligations and honor).

This metaphor represents how adult daughters provide support and stability much like a strong pillar supports a greater structure. Collectivism emphasizes familial unity, high-power distance clarifies defined roles, and high-uncertainty avoidance reflects the importance of predictable family structures. Short-term orientation highlights the immediate significance of familial honor and personal integrity.

A Thread in a Family Tapestry

Cultural dimensions: in-group collectivism (interconnected family roles), gender egalitarianism (emphasis on relational roles, not hierarchy), and uncertainty avoidance (favoring secure, structured relationships).

This metaphor portrays daughters as essential weavers of family cohesion and connectedness. The collectivism dimension foregrounds the importance of close family bonds, while femininity emphasizes emotional intelligence and connection. High-uncertainty avoidance underscores the security provided by tight-knit family bonds, highlighting the daughter's role in maintaining family unity and stability. Adult daughters are an integral part of a family's fabric, woven tightly into the big picture of the extended family bond.

A Guiding Star in the Night Sky

Cultural dimensions: in-group collectivism (devotion to family and group well-being), humane orientation (empathy and nurturing leadership), and future orientation (vision and direction for the future).

The guiding star in this metaphor symbolizes daughters as influential figures who guide family members through life's complexities. Collectivism highlights daughters' commitments to supporting community well-being, and femininity emphasizes relational care, empathy, and interconnectedness. Like a star that guides others through darkness, daughters can lead with emotional strength, wisdom, and clarity. Daughters are valued for guiding and caring for others through various challenges and stages of life as resilient and visionary figures.

A Flame in the Hearth

Cultural dimensions: in-group collectivism (center of family life), humane orientation (nurturing others), future orientation (preserving tradition and legacy), and uncertainty avoidance (providing dependable emotional warmth).

This metaphor portrays daughters as central to the warmth enjoyed by a daughter's family and community. Women often take the lead on nurturing connections and practicing traditions. Collectivism emphasizes communal belonging, femininity underscores nurturing relationships and community bonds, and long-term orientation ensures preservation of rituals across generations. High-uncertainty avoidance means valuing stability, ensuring the continuity of shared values and practices for future generations. In these spaces, women nurture traditions and provide ongoing support for community members.

These metaphors reflect the many ways daughtering and daughterhood are a multiplicity of things: interconnection, responsibility, care, expectation, and love. The GLOBE cultural dimensions help us appreciate the way women from around the world interpret and perform daughterhood unique to their personhood and cultural identity.

Doing daughtering at the intersections of gender, race, sexuality, and many other important social identities means a balancing act for daughters. But you have a choice and a voice, and can resist, embrace, or challenge aspects of daughterhood as you see fit. As a daughter, you hold the power to honor what came before while imagining and building something better for what comes next.

ACTIVITY 5: A NEW TRADITION OF DAUGHTERING

In this activity, you will brainstorm a new family tradition. This tradition may be something you saw a friend do, read about on Pinterest, or maybe it just burst from your own mind. No matter how you put it together, traditions are born in two ways. First, during the event, we *name it and claim it*. This is like saying, "First Annual Daughters' Summer Luncheon." Second, you repeat the tradition within a reasonable time frame. You can have traditions annually or *way* more often than that. Maybe every time family has a camping trip, everyone wears matching PJs. Or each time you go shopping, buy a new flavor of coffee drinks to try. Traditions are what you make them, but they don't start themselves.

Start by thinking about what values are important to you and your family. The following questions may spark some ideas:

What brings your family joy? (e.g., shared meals, outdoor adventures, storytelling)
What values do you want to honor? (e.g., love, gratitude, resilience)
What milestones or special moments deserve recognition? (e.g., turning points, personal achievements)

Keep the brainstorming going by thinking through the various aspects of your new tradition:

What's the purpose? Is your tradition about celebrating, connecting, supporting, or reflecting?

What will it feel like? Some experiences are poignant, others full of energy. Are you someone who wants to be cherished quietly in the coziness of your home or cheered on publicly with a big, splashy Facebook post?

Who will participate? Who do you imagine being involved in your special event? Picture who you want surrounding you, whether it's family, friends, or members of your community.

What will you do? Consider what happens at this event that you want to become a tradition, such as doing a special activity, making a meal, exchanging keepsakes, crafting, or telling campfire stories. For families who live far apart but still want to bond, try making a slide deck called "My Adventures" and present some of your life's recent highlights to everyone over a video chat. Or play synchronous online games together that allow users to join from around the world.

How do you ritualize it? What are the symbols, rituals, or other creative elements that will make this tradition memorable (and more likely to be repeated)? You might light candles, take instant photos, create a time capsule, or exchange handwritten notes.

Fill in the table below to begin architecting your new daughtering tradition.

A NEW TRADITION OF DAUGHTERING	
Thought Prompts	**Responses**
Name of your tradition:	
Purpose this tradition fulfills:	
When (and how often) this will occur:	
Who will be there:	
Activities or rituals:	
Special keepsakes or symbolic items:	

Plan your first tradition by inviting everyone involved and assigning special roles. Celebrate something meaningful to you (again and again)! Remember, even if your event is a virtual one—like cooking a Sunday meal live together or doing karaoke night online from different houses—you can bond with family from anywhere if you put in the intentional effort.

Chapter 6

WHAT DO I OWE?

A DAUGHTER'S JOURNEY OF RESPONSIBILITY

As you get to know yourself better along your daughtering journey, you come to a point where you pause to consider the others you have a responsibility to as a daughter. After all, you can't be a daughter without having (or having once had) a mother and a father. The role of a daughter is one that is in dynamic interplay with parents, stepparents, grandparents, siblings, stepsiblings, in-laws, cousins, aunties or uncles, and your community. But daughtering is also something that you do for yourself and by yourself.

This back-and-forth over who is involved in *my* daughtering can cause a bit of confusion. Is daughtering about the self or is it about the other person who receives my daughtering? So much of what we have already covered shows that being a daughter is social: It's rooted in a social system and the context of where you are daughtering from and who you are daughtering with. So, yes, being a daughter is something that happens in connection with others and in connection with the world around you. So what happens when these two worlds collide? When your parents want more from you, but you are realizing you've reached your limit on how much space daughtering can take up in your life?

When I spoke with Leslie, age 31, she told me about the guilt she was feeling as her parents asked her for more of her time. The past week, she'd gotten a text in the family group reminding her specifically (and not the other three siblings on the thread) that her grandmother's birthday party was coming up and she hadn't yet confirmed she'd be coming. Even though they knew Leslie had a demanding career and a fiancé with whom she wanted to spend time, it seemed like every week she'd get another text, which used phrases like "Family should come first" if Leslie tried to bow out of events. When she told them about having other plans, one of her parents or the other would ask her, "Can't you just reschedule it?"

Leslie told me it was bad enough dealing with the guilt of gently but firmly trying to say no to her parents, or the guilt she felt when she was missing something at work or with her partner; but she also felt as though her sisters were complicit by staying silent. They were on the family group texts and never stood up for her. Sometimes they even sided with her parents.

All of that was hard enough on Leslie; though she had a big, loving family, she felt isolated. But she also felt that she didn't have any friends who understood. She had been venting to girlfriends about her family, but none of them seemed to sympathize. Instead, they further isolated her by making it seem like she was ungrateful. One friend looked over the texts from Leslie's mom and said, "Well, it seems nice that she wants you around." She didn't understand what Leslie was struggling with. But I did. Leslie didn't want to seem ungrateful for parents who loved her and wanted her time, but they were bleeding her dry emotionally. And the message she was getting from her closest people was: "Suck it up and be grateful for what you've got."

That message is a toxic refrain that keeps daughters from being allowed to change, evolve, and individuate. It's not that the people are toxic themselves, but the cultural message to "just deal with it" is one that silences women and forces us into small boxes of acceptable behavior.

I remember when I was a young married person and people used to ask me about my new in-laws, I would say that my only complaint was they loved us too much. My in-laws seemed to want unmitigated access to my husband and me. On the one hand, it was very generous to be taken out to dinner or invited on vacations, but there were invisible strings attached to these offers; we were spending all our time with them (and only them).

As workers, newlyweds, and child-free people, with friends around the world, I yearned to go do other stuff with other people. Or be on a solo adventure with my husband. But it seemed so ungrateful to turn them down, and even worse to be annoyed by their constant attention. It took me many years to learn to build the boundaries around my time without feeling like a bad daughter-in-law.

I can't say I have mastered it, but one thing I learned to embrace was that the tension between choosing myself and choosing another person is part of our daily experience. Without it, we'd feel isolated and unwanted. Too much of that pull and we feel engulfed. And there's science behind that idea.

DIALECTICAL TENSIONS

When I think of the push and pull between a daughter and her parent, I am reminded of relational dialectic theory, a set of propositions about how humans relate, first proposed in the 1990s by communication scholars Leslie Baxter and Barbara Montgomery. They proposed a framework to help understand the different forces in a relationship, like invisible strings that tie you together with another person, tugging you back and forth constantly as you attempt to relate to one another.

The core idea is that relationships are dynamic, meaning there will always be opposing forces you need to manage—not solve. It's kind of like living with two truths that contradict each other but are both valid at the same time. The relational dialectics theory says that at the core of this framework is the notion that meaning-making results out of the struggle of different (sometimes competing) world-views. Your worldview is made up of your outlook on life, the way you value things, and how you foresee the future unfolding.

Worldviews can be in opposition, exerting tensions between two people trying to be in a relationship. These energies that tug back and forth are not problems to be solved; there is no resting place for the "status quo" of opposing forces. Instead, these shifts and changes represent ongoing conversations between people who are changing, growing, and continuing to learn from each other all the time. Nothing about being a daughter is static. You are as dynamic and varied as the spaces you live in and the beautiful messy people you interact with.

Let's explore a few of the classic dialectical tensions that have been identified in all kinds of interpersonal relationships:

Balancing Independence versus Interdependence as a Daughter

As adult daughters, you have probably felt the tension between independence—building your own life and career—and interdependence, keeping up meaningful connection with your family. Prioritizing independence helps you establish a sense of self and allows you to grow into the person you want to be. Setting boundaries protects your time, energy, and well-being, ensuring that your needs are met; but too much independence can end up feeling isolating. Striking the right balance is key.

Healthy interdependence involves choosing fulfilling family interactions rather than performing out of obligation. Emotionally checking in through a text, call, or another small act of care and participating in the rhythms of family life that you cherish can help keep the bond strong. Keep yourself from overdoing it by learning to say no without guilt and reframing family time as an investment in togetherness rather than a duty. Viewing the dialectics of independence and interdependence as complementary forces and not opponents can help you make strategic choices that benefit you and your evolving family.

Openness versus Closedness

When women discuss their innermost circle of trusted allies, which *might* include their family members, they talk about how much they share and how much they keep to themselves. Maybe you've found yourself wondering things like *How much do I tell my mom about my horrible boss at work?* Or *Is it worth it to explain why I am maintaining this boundary?* These moments of reflection are what the dialectical tension of openness versus closedness is all about.

These are instances of decision-making about your life when you decide what to disclose and what to keep private. It's normal to question these things, because intimacy in relationships can grow through sharing about yourself. But it's also true that maintaining privacy can ensure that you are protecting yourself (or others in your circle). Striking the balance can be tricky, especially if you have parents who feel entitled to your private life and sharing that information with anyone and everyone.

Being open is a way to build trust and deepen your connection with a parent. As a daughter, you want your parents to see you for who you are today (not the child you used to be). Disclosing key pieces of information allows your parents to be part of your life. When you share information, you become vulnerable and open yourself up to an abundance of support and affirmation. As you stay open, you can reduce miscommunications because both parties are conveying information clearly.

The risk of being too open, however, is it could lead to unwanted outcomes: Your parents might try to give you unsolicited advice, make it about themselves by sharing a similar story of their own, or take the information and run away with it, exposing your precious private moments to others. If this has happened to you before, it's hard to trust and be open again since there is a risk for judgment or loss of control.

You have the option to promote closedness or privacy around your life, which allows you to maintain full autonomy. Keeping your information to yourself is a form of protection that helps you avoid the unknown responses of your parents, thereby promoting a sense of relief. When you are discreet or private, you can keep things to yourself until you are ready. This works well for individuals who need to sit longer with their experiences to know their own mind until they are ready to share. Being closed with your details can also prevent conflict and reduce the emotional labor of explaining and justifying yourself to your parents.

The risk of being too private, of course, is becoming cold and isolated. Parents can feel shut out and you might miss the benefits of being in a community with older, wiser individuals who love you. The relationship can become disconnected and feel inauthentic in these situations, which benefits no one.

A trend I noticed on social media recently captures this tension perfectly. In these videos, daughters joke about suddenly wanting to spill all their secrets just because they're having a nice meal with their mom. The urge to share is strong, triggered by the familiar comfort of a parent's presence. Yet, there's an underlying hesitation—the knowledge that past reactions weren't always ideal. Some daughters fear judgment, while others worry that their mom may not actually want to hear certain truths. The viral nature of these videos proves that this tension resonates deeply with many women. Some commenters declare, "Nah, I tell my momma everything," while others laugh knowingly at the unspoken risk of oversharing.

Communication privacy management (CPM) theory by Sandra Petronio describes how individuals feel a sense of ownership around their private information, and they decide whether to disclose it based on multiple concerns such as internal privacy rules and the likelihood of the information to cause relational turbulence. What might seem like a trite social media trend actually reveals a fascinatingly complex web of evaluations that daughters make about their private information, their relationship with a parent, and their best guesses at what will happen after an important disclosure.

Finding the sweet spot in the dialectics of openness and closedness that works for you is a balancing act. Some days you may feel eager and open to connect, while other days you decide to draw a line around your space. Remember, the goal is not to choose one or the other, but to find ways to stay in movement between the two goal posts. As an adult daughter, you must learn to trust yourself.

While the process is different for everyone, there are a few steps to trusting yourself that you can rely on. First, listen to your inner voice. That means noticing how you feel and allowing yourself to act accordingly; pause and ask yourself: *What is my body telling me? What feels right?*

Second, set and hold boundaries. Self-trust is strengthened when you honor your own limits. If something doesn't feel right, respect that feeling. There's more work in this area further along in the book.

Lastly, you can be patient with the process. Evolution of self and change in relationships happens so slowly you might think a sloth was whipping past you. But transformation takes time.

The goal with healthy relationships is to be safe and seen but not overexposed. As the saying goes, you don't want your butt hanging out in the wind. But if you're not sure that your parents will cover it for you, you've got to cover it yourself. Whisper to yourself, *I'm connected but I'm still me.* And feel the power of the self-mantra wash over you.

Stability versus Change

When it seems like everything is shifting in a daughter's life, it's natural to cling to some things that you want to stay the same. The dialectic of stability versus change demonstrates our desire for predictability and routine even while we long for the novel and exciting. Relationships flourish with balance: they need a dash of excitement as well as the guarantee of stability. Parents can often expect daughters to keep things the way they've always been, like keeping a family business going or continuing longstanding traditions that require mandatory attendance at a certain place and time. While these pillars of family life can be comforting, it can also be true that you're evolving; daughters grow in unexpected ways that don't always fit into the neat boxes of "the way things have always been done." The comfort of keeping things the same is often opposed with the excitement and challenge of change and opportunity coming your way. While you may not be able to have both in full measure simultaneously, you also don't have to let go of these ideals. Stability creates a sense of security within families and relationships, while change brings growth *and* disruption.

When you lean into the stability of a family, you can maintain routines and create predictable patterns. This is not only safe for daughters, but reassures parents that daughters are not going to leave them and grow beyond the bounds of their understanding. The risk, however, of too much stability is becoming stagnant, tepid, and wearisome. When a daughter allows the legacy to overtake the new, her parents may see the same person they've always known—their little girl—and revert to (or maintain) old patterns of behavior that no longer fit with the grown-up woman she's become. When that happens, resentment can build and make growth and evolution feel impossible for a woman aching to find bold challenges ahead.

Life is, of course, all about change. Even nature will show you that. For daughters in the middle of their lives, there are many new phases to experience in their career, their nuclear families, and even in personal growth (hello the awakening of my 40s!). Change can make you better than who you used to be as you grow past the confines of old roles and into new versions of yourself. Change can open up new doorways that build bridges with your parents, allowing for even deeper bonding than you had imagined possible. And change allows new ideas and traditions to enter the picture, which is especially important when you also consider the grandkids who are pushing and shaping the family as well.

Overdoing the change can be unsettling, both for a daughter and a parent. One or both of you could find a new job and change living arrangements. There could even be a major illness or even a death in the extended family. A new person could enter the family through birth or marriage. Even if you think of yourself as a person who embraces change well, you can look around and start to feel shaky. Rapid shifts to the status quo of your lives can leave you dizzy, anxious, and unsure of whether you like all the newness. Plus constant change can be a lot of work, which leaves little time for the security of rest.

As you manage the same versus the new, you must embrace that both are valuable and necessary. There's not a one-size-fits-all solution, but a negotiation of agreement among the family members who are invested in each other with love.

Given Family versus Chosen Family

You may have thought about your given family before—those connected by birth, marriage, or law versus your chosen family, which includes people you've meaningfully built relationships with and claim as loved ones, despite no blood or legal ties. These relationships might come from your job (ever heard of a "work dad"?), deep friendships (like those attending "Friendsgiving"), or special communities you inhabit (AA peers or LGBTQIA+ allies).

Society often suggests your given family deserves your energy, time, loyalty, money, or care. But many people find deeper affection and belonging outside these traditional boundaries. Emotional fulfillment can come from your chosen family instead of, or alongside, your given family.

A daughter's given family (siblings, bio parents, in-laws, cousins, weird uncles, and others) comes with societal expectations attached. The saying "family comes first" can invoke feelings of obligation or guilt, suggesting you must care for these people because of blood or paperwork. Yet leaning toward your given family can also create a sense of duty to shared history and honor. You learn about your origins and uphold values related to loyalty and legacy. Milestones like birthdays and holidays, though seemingly banal, offer meaningful inclusion.

The risk of overly prioritizing your given family is that you can feel pressure to spend time with people who don't understand or accept you, leading to unease or guilt. There's often an implied (or loudly shouted!) belief that you owe your given family something.

Your chosen family, including friends and neighbors—your village—become significant organically based on shared interests, commitment, and mutual respect. These voluntary connections are often more meaningful because they're chosen rather than chance.

Leaning into your chosen family offers affirming, reciprocal relationships. You build a village of people who genuinely show up during tough times and allow you to express yourself authentically without shame. Yet prioritizing your chosen family can create conflict, with your given family sometimes misunderstanding or feeling jealous, causing internal doubt and feelings of tension between obligation and personal contentment.

You can take steps to enforce your own choices and preferences within your families (both your given family and your chosen one).

Relational dialectic theory (RDT) isn't about solving or fixing relationships; it's about recognizing the ongoing and unseen forces that shape them. These push-and-pull dynamics aren't meant to be resolved but understood, as relationships are constantly in motion, always trying to balance between opposing needs. While it's tempting to want a clear endpoint—a way to "fix" things permanently—RDT challenges us to embrace the fluidity of our most important relationship connections. Importantly, dialectal tensions don't always mean conflict; they can also mean longing, joy, and the deep effort of choosing to be in relationship with others. This ongoing readjustment is not a flaw, but a sign of the vivacity of being in relationship—a complex and beautiful gift of being human.

And most adult daughters are grateful for their role, and happy to have a relationship with their parent or parents, whether now or in the past. There are benefits to receiving familial connection. And there are also hardships. That's the human condition. But for women, often the role you must fulfill is to discuss these relational issues. That's something that has been left out of the conversation until now.

Jennifer, for example, is a 45-year-old daughter who has spent decades managing a challenging relationship with her father. Her dad often made rude, cutting remarks to anyone in his orbit, some of them too out-of-pocket to repeat. Each phone call or family gathering left Jennifer bracing herself for another offhand comment that made her cringe. But the kicker was that whenever she vented her frustrations to her husband, his response was always the same: Yes, your dad is difficult, but let's not rock the boat.

They were in a living situation that was only possible with Jennifer's dad's financial support. And while she was grateful for that opportunity many of her peers didn't get, Jennifer felt trapped, indebted (not gifted), and silenced. She grappled daily with the tension between gratitude and resentment. The friends who knew the intimate details would tell her to ignore it. All of it.

"He's from a different generation," they said. "He's not going to change." And Jennifer felt that maybe they were right. Everyone in her life seemed to be saying that access to boundaries and any feeling of control or normalcy was out of reach for Jennifer. But she knew that she couldn't go on this way. Jennifer may have felt stuck, but she had a lot of options: First, she could talk to her dad directly about how his words hurt her. Even though that conversation might make her anxious, Jennifer could script some statements to use in a call or text if speaking face-to-face was too intimidating. Jennifer could also script some replies to use when her dad was making his colorful remarks. Responding in the moment with a phrase like "I'm going to step away for a bit" could offer her a subtle way to show him that his remarks bothered her without needing to use a rebuke or describe why she feels this way. See the end of chapter 9 for an activity on script-writing.

I'm here to say that change is within your grasp. You can have gratitude to be in connection with your parents as a daughter and also want to speak frankly about the experience. You can be grateful for the people in your lives while also wanting things to improve, for you and for families in the future. You can be happy in at least the eudaemonic sense of being a daughter, yet still yearn for some hedonic happiness changes that would improve your life and the lives of your family members, too.

Change takes time and is a journey. You begin with reflection, move on to planning, take steps toward strategizing, and transition forward with enacting meaningful change. The good news is that you are not forced to pick a side between you and your parents.

You can find a balance along any dialectical tension. You can have a relationship with your parent that is manageable and rewarding. That comes from the internal reflection of the risks and rewards of keeping different people in your life and giving them your time and energy. But you have to know your own value systems and life goals to make these decisions.

WHAT DOES A DAUGHTER OWE ANYONE?

A lot of daughters wonder "So, what do I owe them?" If daughtering is an endeavor both inside a woman and externally in relationship with others, then a daughter can optimize that experience both by finding what fills her up as an individual, while also seeking an understanding of what she owes to her parent(s) or family.

Occasionally, daughters feel like they are fodder for their parents' social lives, or even function as their parents' reason for being. What a big responsibility! Perhaps your parents have their own goals and rich lives filled with meaning, but many women find that their parents are relying on them and trying to live vicariously through them. And this can be a heavy burden to carry, especially if there's any disagreement between parent and daughter about how she ought to live. But you are allowed to ask yourself how much you extend into the lives of your parents and how much they extend into yours, to ask to what degree am I a part of their lives and they a part of mine? How much of me must I give to them?

I'll share an example of a conversation I have had among friends and seen represented in online spaces. But before I share it, I will ask these questions that my friend asked of me after she told me about her experience. By starting with the questions at the beginning, you can ponder your thoughts on these topics as you go along: Am I obliged to participate in my mother's content creation on social media? Should I give in to everything she wants because it's my mom [and I owe her]? If I go along with this, am I abandoning myself? What happens if I make a big deal out of it? Is this a hill I'm willing to die on?

My friend Alma told me she opened Facebook one day because she was planning to sell something on Marketplace. Right at the top she noticed a post from her mom that she was tagged in. Alma was already groaning as she clicked to see what was shared. She began to feel that tightness in her stomach when she looked at an entire album of pictures from the past weekend that her mom uploaded, featuring Alma, her sister, their partners, and the grandkids.

The post gushed over what great parents Alma and her sister are to their kiddos. Of course, that's a nice sentiment, but the over-the-top admiration only makes it harder for Alma to explain why she doesn't want her mom's five-hundred-plus "friends" to have so many private details about their lives. And this, of course, comes on the heels of conversations Alma has already had with her mom about Facebook posts with the grandkids. That time, her mom responded with something like "Oh, it's just harmless fun and I don't understand why you don't like the compliments!" But she had agreed to cut back. And, yes, these new posts were slightly different, but even with having "privacy" settings, Alma believed it was likely the posts could be seen by her mom's gardening group and neighborhood association, too.

The digital oversharing felt like a violation of trust. But what should she do? Of course, her mom is proud of the family and wanted to share details about them out of a sense of excitement and love. Or her mother might be trying to keep up with the neighbors whose grandkids went to fancy private schools and won skiing medals. Alma sighed and knew she would have to call her mother. But she wasn't quite ready for that, because she was sure it would be some kind of battle. And that's the story she brought to me, with the questions above.

When we got to talking, Alma and I discussed how her mom is participating in virtue signaling, or the public act of sending hidden messages to gain social approval. It's like she's saying, "Look what a devoted grandmother I am" or "Family is my top priority" or even more catty, "My kids are better than yours." That kind of messaging can seem inauthentic and false (aside from the inherent security

concerns related to online posts with kids' pictures and other identifying information). Sure, her mom can call this a simple form of
documentation for their lives, but that's what photo albums at your
house are for. Instead, the social media posts project an idealized
version of Alma and her sister, their kids, and their lives, which
is then quite difficult to live up to, whether out in the community
or even as Alma considers what her mom expects from her. These
types of posts also feel invasive to Alma because she loses control of
her image and the representations of her family online. It's like having your identity stolen, but the thief is a good-natured grandma
who swears it's all in good fun.

So, what does Alma do? At minimum, she has a conversation
with her mom and communicates the things she's feeling about loss
of control and projecting a false narrative about their family. Beyond
that, Alma could choose to set a lot more boundaries to protect herself in the future, but there are consequences to the relationship if her
mom cannot (or refuses to) understand the reasoning behind that.

And this is where we pick back up the question about daughtering and how much we need to give. If the social media posts make
Alma uncomfortable, how much is she required to give in to her
mother's actions? And while this is an individual question that requires each daughter to decide for herself, it's important for daughters to know the "hill they're willing to die on." This phrase comes
from military battles where decisions have to be made about when
a skirmish is so important that you're willing to risk everything,
even death, to keep your territory. Confronting a parent, especially
over boundaries, can be especially exhausting and draining. Different people and generations have different value systems, so it's very
likely Alma's mom will disagree with her attitude toward these posts.
But each daughter comes to decisions like this one with their parent
where they must ask themselves if they feel deeply enough about the
issue at hand to tackle the problem, knowing that it might cause tension, hurt feelings, or even lasting change in the relationship.

When Alma asked for my genuine response to this issue, I began by asking a few key questions to help her decide if this is her

"hill" or if she might be able to let it go. (After all, she needs to know her opinion and not mine, so I acted more as a facilitator.) First, I asked her, "What's at stake for you if this behavior continues?" Alma's response was that the unknown of future posts and the escalation of the intensity and distribution of information was causing her a lot of anxiety and frustration that continued long after the post was made, as she anticipated the next time the "other shoe would drop" or her mother would do something unexpected. In short, what was at stake for her was existing in a tense state of unknowing and discomfort.

Next, I asked Alma, "Can you let this go without resentment?" She told me that, yes, she felt like she could let the issue go without resenting her mom, but only because she was positive that her mom's motives were good and kind. This wasn't a situation where a parent is purposely trying to needle or undermine their child or seize control over the way a grandkid is being raised. It was more about the identity of her mom and how Alma felt used to propel a certain narrative in the world. All in all, it wasn't *that* bad. But it did annoy her and she disliked it.

Okay, I continued, "What are the potential consequences?" Well, she told me, the consequences of telling her mother how she really feels about the situation is that she risks some bad or awkward feelings with her. She predicted there might be some tension or even a few days of no phone calls while her mother processed being upset. It wasn't likely to be a big blowup, but Alma never enjoyed upsetting her mother.

Lastly, I asked, "Is there a middle ground?" She thought about it for a bit and then responded, "Yes." The middle ground, according to Alma, would be asking her mother again to stop the online posts, but would not include a deep dive on what Alma thought about her mother's actions. And, she said, another tactic would be creating a better awareness of pictures being taken in the moment and trying to prevent a future social media love parade by catching the picture-taking in its tracks. Alma decided she would be both reactive and proactive.

And while you might read that story and decide to choose a very different reaction (it's like a Choose Your Own Adventure book!), this processing and new direction was satisfactory for Alma. She preserved her relationship with her mom without abandoning her values. But she was not (at least not yet) going to have a big argument over this issue since she understood her mother was acting out of a loving motive. And that was going to be "good enough" for today. The last I heard about this issue, Alma had taken steps to talk to her mother about the posts, taking a new tactic that we hadn't even discussed. Instead of telling her mom what to do or even what she wanted to see as an outcome Alma decided to focus on their shared values, telling her mom that she really wanted to prioritize the safety of her kids—and that meant in the online world, too. When she talked about her fears, it "unlocked" something in her mom, who started to see them as being on the same team and cut back on the volume of shared pictures.

DAUGHTERING BELONGS TO ME

There are no hard-and-fast rules for how daughters must behave. And if you begin to see or feel that these invisible bars are closing in around you, it's your job to fight back against the rigid expectations. All daughters are doing daughtering. Showing love and care happens in the accumulation of tiny moments over time. Daughtering happens with what you do with your hands, but also in your hearts and minds.

You can trust that your efforts are sufficient for preserving the relational bonds, while also protecting your autonomy. You cannot escape daughtering, as it touches all parts of your life, becoming fundamental to who you are and how you make decisions, but you can allow yourself to evolve as a daughter. Even when it's uncomfortable to be in a growing phase, you can make adjustments that create a positive impact. And every adjustment you make shows the world that daughters are agents of change within family systems.

Being a daughter is not separate or split from the most basic part of yourself. Being a daughter is part of your identity; it's a piece you carry with you whether in very big ways or small. If I haven't felt or noticed this before, it is likely because of the invisibility of daughtering and the ways it has been obscured from the social consciousness.

I believe that when I come to embrace the daughter inside me, among me, through me, and as integral to my daily life, I begin to consider how I can find balance between being me versus being a daughter for them. Because as much as daughtering is within me, it is also an act of giving that incorporates others. So, if daughtering is part of me forever, how do I make the right decisions about how to do daughtering at any given time?

ACTIVITY 6: WHAT'S MY DAUGHTERING BATTERY LEVEL?

This activity helps you reflect on your energy, emotional reserves, and resources to better understand your capacity for daughtering today. The goal is to gauge how much energy you have available and how much you are currently expending—giving you a clearer picture of when to say yes, no, or not now to daughtering tasks.

Our batteries can be full or drained. Rate yourself on each of these energies to determine your overall battery level.

WHAT'S MY DAUGHTERING BATTERY LEVEL?		
	Energies	**Battery Level, 1–10**
1	Physical energy—health, sleep, fitness	
2	Mental energy—workload, stress, sharpness	
3	Emotional energy—relationships, family dynamics, bullshit tolerance	
4	Community energy—volunteering, neighboring, engaging online	
5	Personal energy—rest, hobbies, self-care, balance	
	Total Daughtering Battery Volume	____ / 50

After rating yourself on each energy level, add up your total score to find your Daughtering Battery Level.

SCORING

41+: Charged Up and Ready to Do Daughtering

Your battery is charged up and eager for the opportunities ahead. You're capable, steady, and ready to do daughtering without depleting your reserves. You may feel like you're able to meaningfully contribute daughtering acts to your family and community, while staying in balance with your own well-being. Be sure to protect your energy to stay well charged for the long term.

25–40: Managing but Monitoring

Your battery is at a normal level for a busy woman. You are functional and juggling all your responsibilities but must continue to monitor your battery levels. Daughtering tasks might get done but sometimes can feel like a drain on your already strained resources. This is a good time to ask for help, delegate where you can, and make time for small moments of recovery. Let's be real: You may never reach 100 percent capacity, but you can be a healthy, functional daughter at this reserve level.

5–24: Critical Levels—Find an Outlet to Plug Into

Your battery is getting low. You may feel overwhelmed, depleted, or stretched thin. At this level, even small daughtering tasks can feel impossible. This is a signal that you need to find an outlet to plug into and recharge before committing to more responsibilities. It's okay to step back, set firm boundaries, and prioritize your well-being. Think of it as giving yourself permission to recharge so you can be at 100 percent soon.

Monitoring your social battery can provide an awareness for when it's time to go, slow down, or be a no-show as a daughter in your relationships. You are the only one who knows what it feels like to live inside your life, but a tool like battery awareness can help manage your capacity intentionally, keeping your efforts sustainable over time.

Chapter 7

WHO MY PARENT IS NOW
(AND WHY THAT MATTERS)

Daughters have their parents for a lifetime—not only the length of time that our parents are alive, but also the length of our own lifetime. A hallmark of daughtering is its constancy in your life as part of your identity from birth to death. Another hallmark is change, the never-ending update that occurs as child and parent age and develop over a lifespan.

As a daughter, you can either feel stuck in the past, imagining your parent the way they used to be, or you can get nervous about the future. This is also true for the daughter whose parent is no longer with her through circumstances like death, estrangement, or myriad other reasons. So, you've got a yesterday, today, and perhaps also a tomorrow version of your parent. It can be tough to know how to best interact with the parent you have *right now*, in the flux of changing experience.

This chapter provides a framework for understanding our evolving relationship with our parents as they age. There's information here for the daughter who can't stop thinking about tomorrow and who your parent (or you) will be at some point in the future. And there's stuff here for the daughter whose parent is no longer present, but you can still feel the connection and some kind of relationship with them. This chapter is for those who see something shifting under their feet but can't quite name it or hold on to it. But perhaps, like me, you want to avoid a future of regret by staying in the present moments of your life with the daughtering experience you have today.

THE KINSHIP SHIFT

I have recently had some conversations with peers that went like this: "Who *are* these people? My parents would never have [voted/paid/traveled/bought] like that before. I am having trouble recognizing them now. It has totally surprised me to see them [insert previously not-done thing that is now commonplace for the aging parent]."

And then others chime in to tell *their* stories of how their parents seem totally different now than the way they used to be. One of my sister's friends, Ellen, told her about a change in her mom's cleaning habits. When Ellen was growing up, her mother was a clean freak. Every Saturday, they did hours of deep cleaning, including baseboards, refrigerators, behind the washer and dryer, everything. Now, when Ellen visits her mom's house, there's dust and grime.

She wonders, *Has her eyesight changed? Can she not see it?* Or maybe, Ellen mused, my mom is aging and it's too difficult for her to clean the same way. But Ellen says her mom appears to be in good health and pretty spry when playing with the grandkids. And, Ellen wondered, if she's simply decided not to do the cleaning herself, why not go ahead and hire a service to come and clean? Or perhaps her mom had been inhabited by an alien who likes dust, Ellen pondered, because this version of her mom seems *so* different from the "before" version.

Yes, Ellen's mom has changed. And your mom has changed. You may even find yourself asking, "Who is this person?" when you interact with your parent. Your brain is attuned to the status quo and finds it challenging to loosen your grip on past labels and understandings, when you believe you've already figured it out. But this is where you have a growth opportunity: noticing the changes in your parent and accepting them as the new way, with no going back. You're now inside the *kinship shift*.

SHADES OF THE SHIFT

The kinship shift is a term used to describe the experience of moving from a time when your parent was an independent, fully autonomous, self-sufficient adult to a relational stance where they need more love, respect, and care from you.

The kinship shift is my term for the "before" times of the parent you once knew with the "later" times when your parent needs you to lead the way. You remember a time, whether it was from your childhood or in your young adult years, when your parent was in charge. You naturally depended upon a parent for food, shelter, finances, and even legal decisions. For many daughters, this sense of "parent in charge" continues into adulthood, and you remember a time when your parent was the one capably leading the way. Your parent seemed to be the "decider" in relational matters between you, and you deferred to their wishes. You may still be in this space now.

But then there comes a shift, a transition time. The changes in your relationship could be rather sudden or occur over years. On the other side of the shift, you are now the one who runs the relationship. You're in charge, whether you want to be or not.

You can think of the kinship shift as having phases—a before, during, and after. In the times before the shift starts, daughters are aware that the changes to the relationship, especially regarding caregiving, will one day come. Perhaps you've seen it with your aging grandparents or observed as your friends entered that phase of life with their parents. In this phase, you can see what changes may occur but they haven't yet happened. Importantly, the greater awareness you have of your daughtering now and in the future, the more you are continuing to lean into the identity part of daughtering. Here, daughtering may be more thinking and identity related than task or emotion driven.

START OF THE SHIFT

The kinship shift is gradual, sometimes even glacial. And before it even starts, women are aware that it will eventually come. Psychologist Bethany Webster, author of *Mother Wound*, writes about beliefs women have, especially around relationships with their mothers. One concept she shares is that of the maternal horizon. This refers to the way adult daughters envision their future roles and responsibilities regarding their mothers as they age. The horizon line that a young adult woman sees in her future is a liminal space, a figurative way of conceptualizing oncoming changes to the daughter-parent dynamic. It is the point at which daughters anticipate the increasing needs or dependence of their mothers. While this particular term refers to mothers, adult daughters could adopt its usage and apply it to fathers as well, who, though different, often need similar attention from their adult children.

A lot of adult daughters in their 20s and 30s talk to me about a time they know is coming when their parent will need more daughtering. Some even look forward to it. Lottie, age 31, told me: "As she grows older, I think about our relationship—I will become more of the caregiver. She has always been such an excellent caregiver, that I have her as a good example. I am already getting little opportunities to do that. When her dog died, I was able to be there for my mom the way she has always been there for me. I'll have more opportunities to repay that. I'm looking forward to that time because I feel as though my mom has done so much for me. I look forward to watching her grow old and needing me to help her. I look forward to having the opportunity to repay her for all the things she has done for me." What Lottie's comments showed me is that she's been thinking about how to be a daughter in the future but knows that it's not quite the time yet to do daughtering in that way. She's still on the "before" side of the kinship shift.

Another daughter told me that she dreads the day her mom will need more help, because then she'll have to talk to her. Amelia, 42, said, "I know one day she'll really need me, and I'll be dragged back into all her drama. But there's nobody else, so it will have to be me." Again, Amelia recognizes that she's not needed as a caregiver yet, but she anticipates a time when that dynamic will shift.

Even daughters who have yet to experience changes in their parents that would increase daughtering responsibilities can envision a time when that will likely happen. Whether you've noticed your mom caring for your grandpa or great-grandma, or you've read a book with a similar story, or even heard it on the news, it is the reality of daughters that we anticipate our responsibilities decades in advance.

So, it is no surprise that as we anticipate the shift, we attempt to name and define it for ourselves, reducing the uncertainty we may feel in the future. Here's where we get into the trickiness of language. From my many interviews, I have heard women call this shifting, transitional experience a "role reversal." Whenever I picture that, my brain goes to movies like *Freaky Friday* or *Like Father, Like Son* where the child wakes up in the parent's body and vice versa. Of course, role reversal as a concept is not like that, but it is equally fantastical to imagine that daughters and their parents could ever actually switch roles or reverse the aging and experiences they have had thus far in life.

According to human development and family sciences scholar Karen Fingerman, the concept of role reversal oversimplifies the complexities of children and parents in adult intergenerational relationships aging together. Even as a parent's needs may change over time and the power dynamics in the relationship adjust, a parent typically retains their decision-making power and autonomy. That means even if you, as the daughter, feel you're the one "in charge" in your relationship with a parent, there are still limitations and you're not completely in control.

Likewise, many people have tried to describe their relationship with a parent by saying, "Now I'm the parent" or "I'm mothering them now." However, for this to be true, according to Fingerman, a daughter would have to fully take on *all* parenting status and functions, with the parent assuming the role of a total dependent; this doesn't happen to the extent necessary for the saying to be a truism. Many elderly individuals live full, independent lives all the way up until the day they die, retaining the respect of their family, control over their body, finances, and more.

Contrast that with an infant who is cared for by a parent. On the first day of their lives, they are helpless and completely dependent on their parent. Despite changes between daughters and their aging parents, the emotional connection and the history they share cannot be swapped. There's no Uno Reverse card here.

Rather, the daughter will always be the daughter. The parent will always be the one to give the genetic material, provide the maternal home, be older, and have lived through a time period when the daughter was not present. Both father and mother have something the daughter does not. They give it to her through their genetics and their care of a weaker, needier creature at her birth. Poignantly, writer Adrienne Rich articulated the intense relationship between daughters and their mothers this way: "The cathexis between mother and daughter—essential, distorted, misused—is the great unwritten story. Probably there is nothing in human nature more resonant with charges than the flow of energy between two biologically alike bodies, one of which has lain in amniotic bliss inside the other, one of which has labored to give birth to the other."

What Rich is describing is that a mother and daughter can never reverse their roles. And yet, as Rich alludes to, there is so much unknown and unwritten about the daughter-parent relationship because of its invisibility. As the nature of adult family members changes, there's both simultaneous admiration and concern for one another. The parent may seem more vulnerable than they have ever been before, while still retaining their hierarchical position in the family system. A better way to consider how roles change over a lifetime is through the concept of role expansion.

We have talked about how roles morph and transform over a lifetime, but they can also expand. According to role expansion theory, any role (mayor, manager, son, or daughter) can take on new and multiple responsibilities. This could be a drain, but it could also create new fulfillment and even expanded energy for performing the role. Karen Fingerman has shown in her research that a daughter's role can accumulate new features or duties, but that women are able to flex over time and roll with the punches. Just because our roles expand, we can keep calling this daughtering; there's no need to switch terminology. Daughters don't suddenly start doing mothering, but simply become more qualified daughters. And, most important, even though the daughtering job duties may increase, it doesn't signify that we're burdened by the extra work.

Kinship and the work of doing family is necessary and important. Here, kinship refers to relationships—by blood, marriage, adoption, or anything else—that form the basis of family life. These networks are firmly welded together through the work of family members kinkeeping the bonds strong.

Daughters taking on more responsibilities in our roles do so because there's a need and we can handle it. And we even benefit from it, by creating tight-knit families that can rely on each other. Plus, daughters can expect others to do the same for them in the future. That's the feeling of generativity, or paying it forward into the next generation. Adaptations to our role expansion are not, however, totally straightforward. There's a lot to get used to as the kinship shift keeps progressing.

MIDDLE OF THE SHIFT

The next phase of the kinship shift is the very eye of the storm, the most confusing, sometimes heartbreaking part of the shift. It can seem as though your perspective on your relationship with your parent is blurry and confusing. You might see the subtle changes and your parent does not. The middle of the kinship shift can be long and taxing.

Bethany Webster, a psychologist, also said that the maternal horizon is reached when "a daughter's emotional and psychological growth, experience, and success surpasses the capacity and opportunities of her mother." This experience can be tumultuous and tense for the daughter who grieves that her mother cannot, or will not, come with her to new heights. And Webster goes on to say that these changes can cause tension in the relationship, as the mother unconsciously grieves her lack of opportunity or as the mother tries to force the daughter into old patterns.

What's more, a parent who is left behind may find it difficult to cheer for the daughter going on ahead. And the daughter may be sad, and feel guilt and shame, at exceeding or surpassing the parent in some way. The shift can be both normal and natural, while also causing us to experience grief, sadness, and loss of the parent we once had. That can happen even while the parent is living and breathing right in front of us.

The middle of the kinship shift can be frightening for women because we never know when it will occur or how long the tense moments will last. Some women may notice that the shift happens along developmental lines. As your parent ages, their body and mental capacity diminishes, though very subtly.

In *Being Mortal*, gerontologist Atul Gawande describes aging as a gradual decline in physical function, with signs that we may not even be aware of. Beginning in your 30s and 40s, the body begins to exhibit subtle losses in muscle mass, endurance, and vision. By your 50s, joint stiffness, slower metabolism, and cardiovascular risks become more apparent. But it is in your 60s where natural aging begins to accumulate to such a degree that you make different choices and lean on others for support.

In the 60s and beyond, muscle loss accelerates, healing slows, and the risk of chronic illness, fractures, and cognitive decline increases. Gawande's guidance provides clarity that can help you set your expectations for normal aging, both for yourself and your parents. But more important, Gawande takes an approach to mortality that I find refreshing. We each get just the one life to live and we can address our development and aging by considering other approaches beyond medical intervention. Gawande advocates for a holistic approach to aging and living the latter third of your life by prioritizing independence, dignity, and quality of life over mere longevity.

I provide Gawande's perspective on the inevitability of mortality not to point at illness or decline, but rather to note that most adults in family relationships (30s and older) are in the same boat of gentle yet gradual change in our faculties. Only in your late teens and 20s are you an adult who is *gaining* in strength and mental acuity.

This is important to point out because it is not that daughters are "gaining" while their parents are "losing" abilities, but rather the life stage we are at determines our needs, physically at least. According to life-stage researcher and psychologist Erik Erikson, individuals typically progress through eight stages of universal development over a lifetime. Some scholars have suggested that the last four stages of life (adolescence, young adulthood, middle adulthood, and maturity) are mostly a repetition of the first four stages (infancy, early childhood, preschool, and school age). In this model, we as humans develop and progress, but as we age, our development regresses in some ways. While we gain wisdom in elderhood, we lose autonomy. Although we gain respect and perhaps authority as we age and have generations of offspring come after us, we lose physical capabilities. It's a vexing juxtaposition.

Still other research shows that aging is associated with increases in worldly knowledge and wisdom as well as emotion regulation. These are the hallmarks of "adulting" and further support Fingerman's argument that the aging parent with increasing needs is dissimilar from an infant with enormous needs, little agency, and no autonomy.

I'll share a story with you that will allow me to illustrate the kinship shift. I spoke with a woman named Season who told me a few years ago that her mother, who was in her early 70s, had started to seem *different*. Very gradually, she noticed changes in her mom's thinking and processing. Of course, her mom was aging and had a few health concerns, but the striking difference about her mom, according to Season, was her ability to hold a conversation and react with the expected and trusted responses they had shared for decades.

The once deep and vulnerable conversations they had were no longer the same. Her mom had a shorter attention span and didn't always grasp the details of her work life that she was sharing. Season often felt as though her mom would try to start a conversation in an awkward way, bringing up something vulnerable or private, but in front of a few family members. The *old version* of Mom never did that, she said.

On the other hand, Season told me, her mom was in good health and living independently. She had been checked out by multiple doctors and this wasn't a sign of dementia or something wrong. It was just . . . aging. Season's mom was not feeble or frail or anywhere near needing a caregiver or moving to a nursing home. But it was the start of something. And Season didn't know what that was until over five years later.

Little by little, bits and pieces of her mom's personality and routine shifted. It was the small things that Season noticed they lost in their relationship. Season lost trust in sharing her vulnerable parts not because she didn't love her mom, but because she couldn't guess what her mom would say (or to whom) at any given moment. One day, she was reflecting on this *new mom* and it hit her: they had gone through the kinship shift.

For those daughters who have great relationships with their parents, spending time together, discussing your lives, having a mutually beneficial relationship, the onset of the kinship shift can feel disorienting. It's just as sad as a parent raising a teenager and seeing how, within a short, five-ish-year span, they go from teens to young adults. One day they need you to set the boundaries, and soon after, they need you to let go. The reverse effect is true for our parents.

Of course, it really sucks when we don't like this new version of our lives or the "new Mom." Or maybe we do like her, but we just recognize that she's a totally different version from the "old Mom" who was younger and had different capabilities. The love and relationship are no less important than they were previously, but the style of interaction has now changed.

They've changed. You've changed. So why is it hard for us to picture a new version of someone in our lives rather than a static representation of the past? One theory that may help us understand this desire to stay stuck on a version of your mother is the concept of static selves. This psychological framework describes the human tendency to perceive others, particularly our family members, through fixed or unchanging narratives that resist adaptation over time. For adult children, we find ourselves stuck on a vision of our parents despite evolving needs, capabilities, and identities that we experience as we age.

One reason for this is the fixed lens of childhood memory. The parent we had during our formative years stays encapsulated and "frozen in time." We can, without realizing it, have a vision of our parent as the authority figure, caregiver, and a source of emotional and physical security.

We are often resistant to change, especially where it relates to the people in our life who help us feel secure, seen, and known. We resist acknowledging the vulnerability of our parents and the effects of the passing of time. We prefer to stick with our ingrained perception of our parent as strong, capable, or independent. Reconciling who our parent is today is challenging because it can stir up a lot of feelings.

Season told me that her predominate feeling surrounding her mom was frustration, because everything was different, and yet nobody would acknowledge the changes. But underneath those fleeting feelings, she said, was a deep sense of grief and loss. The parent she had known for most of her life was gone—is gone. And yet, the conundrum exists, because she's still here. Season's mother lives independently, does her own bills and grocery runs, takes herself to the doctor. How is her mother both here and gone?

That's the difficulty of being in the middle of the shift. You might feel disoriented while you're in the process of shifting relational decision-making, but you can recognize it once you're on the other side.

THE GROUND HAS SHIFTED

The final phase of the kinship shift is looking back and seeing that things are truly different. You are more in charge than you ever imagined you would be. And when you find your way out of the kinship shift, you look back over how your relationship used to be and it's now clear that you have a parent who is more reliant on you for care, guidance, nurturance, or even task-based help.

This process, traveling across the kinship shift, and the completion of the transition, is what researchers call reaching filial maturity. *Filial* is a word that means "coming from a son or daughter" to a parent, and maturity refers to the completion of development as an adult child. Filial maturity is a dynamic state of doing the normal, daily parent care experienced by middle-aged children. In short, filial maturity is achieved when adult children embrace the parent need as real and actualized then incorporate more parent care into their routine lives.

There are critical transitions in our lives that occur for some but not all women. Think about a phase like adolescence: Most of us stumble through it and come out on the other side, but some people get stuck and never seem to achieve emotional maturity beyond their teen years. These emotional and developmental transitions are different than biological features of aging but thinking about them can reveal a new way to conceptualize what daughters are going through.

A similar developmental phase is called *matrescence*, coined in the 1970s by an anthropologist to describe the transition women experience as they enter motherhood. During matrescence, a woman's body and brain prepare for her new mothering role. It's an all-encompassing transformation with emotional, social, physical, and cultural changes. When a woman becomes a mom, her whole being is different. To get through this transformative period, anticipatory and new moms reach out to their support systems, relying on advice from their mothers, friends, family, and their doctors. Advocates for the concept of matrescence say that spreading awareness about this high-pressure life stage could lead to improvement in maternal mortality rates, reduce racial disparities, and increase access to paid leave. Using this term helps people understand how much women really go through to become mothers.

I think we could borrow this advocacy strategy and when describing the final push through the kinship shift where daughters are called on to step into primary responsibilities in families. This is *daughterescence*. It's a time when women face expanded responsibilities, have a need for increased support, and feel an impact that's both personal and cultural across all spheres of their lives. Daughterescence, the process of becoming the one who leads in the family, is taking on daughtering in a whole new way. You're letting go of the old ways of doing things with your parents and recognizing the new realities of daughterhood. Daughterescence is the culmination of completing the kinship shift, from the before to the after.

The process of achieving daughterescence is as varied as the population going through it. It is as varied as matrescence might be for a 20-year-old woman or a 40-year-old adoptive parent. And these differences make it no less true that you are experiencing the same phenomenon of changing and expanding your role. Likewise, we can expect some typical needs, like increased community support from friends and neighbors, physicians who ask about emotional and physical stressors, and financial brains who assist with the new realities of the family's finances during this change.

While the kinship shift and daughterescence may occur at any age, to different degrees or intensities, the reality is that daughters commonly experience this transition with parents over a long time in a typical life course. Especially for aging parents, daughters have been shown to be the most involved adult child in their elderhood. In short, we're experiencing the kinship shift for many years.

Using the right language to describe our changing daughtering can only help the world to better conceptualize it. For daughters, calling a spade a spade helps us accept it and turn our attention to finding healthy ways to do our role effectively. There is still so much unknown, or *silent*, about a daughter's story, as Adrienne Rich says, but we can make a difference by sharing the spark that allows others to get curious about what we're going through.

WHO'S THE ALPHA?

As I dug into the kinship shift, I began asking a question that I believed would cut to the heart of the matter. After an hour-long interview with participants all about doing daughtering, I would ask, "Between you and your mom, who is the alpha?" When I asked women this question, I was looking for a term that might sum up the power distribution within a relationship. Different from how much you *love* your mother, determining who has the power to influence the other can reveal important insights into relationships.

And I got a lot of surprising answers. Some women vehemently responded to my question: "Me. I'm the alpha." And among those, there were two camps. One group said they had become the alpha very early in life, as late teens or even as a child. Others said that they recently had become the alpha. These daughters are confident and assured of their dynamic in the daughter-mother relationship. They have achieved daughterescence and are on the exit ramp of the kinship shift.

Another group of women, when asked who is the alpha, gave responses like "She is. My mom is the alpha." These individuals shared that this is all they remember since childhood and, in some ways, their mother's power has a choke hold over them. They are in a state of persistent seeking, attempting to please their mother, or level the playing field somehow. These women have not yet achieved daughterescence. And perhaps they never will (although this topic would greatly divert us from the key point at hand, it's worthy of more conversation at a later date).

The final group of women replied to the question about relationship dynamics by telling me, "Oh, my mom is the alpha. But wait, hmm, I think it's really me. But in a subtle way." And it is this final group I found the most interesting. These women heard my question and had an immediate gut response. But, upon some introspection, they shifted. Women who gave these answers described having a longtime alpha mom. Some stories the women told were about their mom's controlling ways and others were about distant and cold relationships.

These women realized the many ways they wielded power in the relationship, mainly via boundaries and self-control. By not allowing their mother to have every piece of them, dictate their behaviors, or negatively impact their moods, they were taking back control. But subtly, perhaps even surreptitiously, so mom never needed to see it.

There are lots of ways to achieve daughterescence and complete the kinship shift and still maintain a relationship with your parents. Personalities, after all, are another important aspect to consider in relationships. What I was most interested in when I asked the alpha question was not making the women *prove* the truth of their response but instead try to understand how they positioned themselves in relation to their parent, and how that impacted their decision-making about interacting with them.

While some of the women described a power balance that shifted much earlier in life, most women I have spoken to, however, had a more measured experience, without high-highs or low-lows. They said that recent developments, in middle adulthood, impacted how they answered this question. This shows yet another way that our relationships change—power shifts between individuals at different times, and both may not even know it.

GETTING GRUMPIER?

In some of my interviews with women in their 30s, 40s, and 50s, there have been many comments that their parent seems to be getting grumpier as they age. And we have discussed why this is happening, with a lot of theories thrown around. Many women give reasons that are relevant only to their mom's specific situation. And yet, I saw a theme.

I came across a Reddit post on this very topic. A Redditor asked on a page for millennials, "Has anyone else noticed their parents becoming really nasty people as they age?" They went on to describe their baby boomer parents who are in their 70s as increasingly isolated and socially combustible. In the 1.2K responses on the post, there was a resounding cry of agreement from the audience of millennial-aged adult children (individuals born 1981–1996 approximately). Those in agreement said that their baby boomer-aged parents (those born 1946–1964) were behaving in ways that saddened and surprised them, including having a lack of empathy, showing entitlement, or being judgmental. The responses blamed the grumpiness on cognitive decline and aging bodies, overuse of social media by boomers, a lack of "doing the work" in therapy, and more.

But why, according to science, do parents change? The socio-emotional selectivity theory (SST) offers one explanation: Older people care a lot less about what the general public thinks of them, and they tighten the net around themselves, trying to pull in their closest friends and family. According to SST, as we age, but especially when we're old, we think of our time in life becoming limited. The more we think that time is running out, the more our social networks and emotional goals evolve to match. As our parents get older and realize they have less time left to live, they prioritize different things. According to SST, older people start to prioritize their close relationships and seek emotional fulfillment from these people. That can explain why daughters may feel like our parents are tightening a net around us—they kind of are.

Another part of SST that's relevant is that as we age, we prune our social connections, dropping people and activities that don't suit our needs. Maybe you've seen your parent stop attending their poker club or girls' nights, which worries you. However, according to the theory, your parent likely dropped this social event because it wasn't fulfilling. Instead, your parent has decided to put their laser focus on you. It's like a hawk staring you down. It's bittersweet, because when you think about your parent wanting more time and investment with you, it might seem like a good thing, but the reality of it can be quite hard.

So, you're not wrong that your parent is likely changing as they age, because we all are. But when you notice your parent acting fussy and disgruntled, it can become like a blockage between you, making it hard to like and get along with them. Maybe this is happening to you: Your parent's pessimism is increasing, and you find them difficult to be around. First, you try to help them change or ignore it, but their behavior is very annoying or even painful. You long for the parent you used to have. So you cope with the sadness by distancing yourself physically or emotionally.

On the Reddit page, some commenters turned reflective, saying that maybe their parent is not the one who's changing the most, but as we increasingly see them through the eyes of an adult, we are changing as well. Whether it's our parent or we who have changed, how we perceive our parent impacts what we think of them, and thus, what we can do about it. So, the question is whether your parent is grumpier—or are you? The source matters because it changes how we approach the problem.

You could see this as an issue of your parent needing to change, you making a change, or the whole situation needing to change. The easiest of these to control, of course, is you. You can start the process of aligning today's version of you with today's version of your parent by recalibrating your expectations of what's possible.

If you struggle to reconcile a past version of your mom or dad with the current version, you're not alone. Known as cognitive anchoring, humans experience this psychological phenomenon when we "anchor" information from our past knowledge bank to make decisions today. It describes how our initial perception or understanding of someone strongly influences how we continue to perceive them, even when evidence of change emerges.

This cognitive shortcut makes it challenging to update our perceptions, resulting in frustration or disappointment when the individual deviates from our expectations. Or, even when we are presented with information about how our parent is changing, we can delay or avoid accepting it and adapting to it ourselves. This is because we prefer stable, predictable relationships.

Interestingly, research on satisfaction over a lifespan has shown a U-shaped curve where younger adults are the most satisfied in their lives, then satisfaction dips in your 40s and 50s, then rises again in your 60s and 70s. Most scholars agree this is due to the intense demands on your time in middle adulthood. But I wonder if it's also because we simply haven't yet adjusted our expectations to ourselves and others changing around us. When we choose to let go of the past versions of ourselves and our parents, we are better able to moderate our time and energy by facing what *is*.

Stability bias is our tendency to believe that people, including ourselves, remain relatively unchanged over time. What can I say, we *really* dislike change. We underestimate how much personality, behavior, attitudes, and emotional states can evolve, particularly during life transitions such as retirement. Because of stability bias, when we notice new or unexpected behaviors from our parents, we often react with surprise, confusion, or even annoyance—because these behaviors don't align with our long-held beliefs about who our parents "should be."

These concepts matter for you because you have already recognized that something—or someone—needs to change in your relationship. And you're also recognizing that both of you already have. Armed with a plan to explore who you are today and the parent you have today, you can make decisions for tomorrow.

WHY DO THE TODAY VERSUS TOMORROW MATH?

We sometimes struggle to reconcile today me with tomorrow me, failing to recognize how we are subtly changing over time. As we have new experiences, we may forget to reassess who we have become. Similarly, we do the same with our parents, not realizing that they have also experienced transition. I think of our identity work as a kind of internal math where we add the new building blocks and drop away the old ones we don't want or need to keep.

Scholars say that identity is a construction of the *self* as it relates to our place in social groups. We form identities by assigning meaning from experiences, then do an internal recalculation of ourselves as we add in new building blocks to our identity or take some away. Adding roles and identities might seem stressful, but research has shown that holding multiple roles generally enriches women's lives by providing purpose, helpful models for behaviors, and positive social feedback. As you take on new roles—worker, friend, mom, wife, caregiver, daughter-in-law, sister-in-law, business owner—you incrementally reshape your self-conceptions. We bring our identities to every moment of our lives, every role we play, and even create brand-new ones in the moment.

We know who we are in any given moment, and we can see who our parent is today; but if we forget to notice the *differences* in how far we've come from the past to the present, that's when we can experience problems. It's up to us to do that internal identity math for ourselves and our parent. When the differences add up to a big sum, we must stop and see how that math works out and take a new approach for the today and future versions of ourselves and our parent. Approaching our relationships as though we're dealing with a new person can give a fresh perspective on how to make it work most effectively.

MY MISSING PARENT

This part of the book is for the daughter who has a hole in her life where a parent should be. Whether your parent is absent, deceased, missing, or estranged, this section is for you. A *missing parent* who you have not been in regular connection with may be out of sight, out of mind, but of course *you still have a parent*. What do I mean? Daughters whose parents have died, are estranged, missing, or not in communication are still daughters. That means your role counterparts (mom or dad) are still figureheads in your mind, even if you are not around them.

Earlier in this book, I shared how daughters can do daughtering even as part of their identity within themselves, meaning, a parent doesn't need to be around or in contact for a daughter to feel like a daughter or own that part of her identity. For those daughters, the construction of their identity as a daughter must use a placeholder as a stand-in for the missing parent. That placeholder may be either a memory or a mental image of who you imagine your parent might be. This imagined caricature of your parent could be cobbled together from stories you've heard or a version of what you think an ideal parent should act like.

The mental image in your head is likely anchored to either a moment in time or the image you've created. You're remembering a parent as they were before they left or imagining the parent you wish you had. While you don't have an opportunity to talk directly to your parent now, there are other ways to communicate your daughtering. That can be through your identity, sharing stories and memories about your parents with friends, or even by having a one-sided conversation with your invisible parent. I know I've had my fair share of conversations with my deceased grandmother by simply looking upward and talking to her, though she never says anything back.

Imagined interactions are cognitions—or thoughts—we have where we imagine an interaction with another person and therefore experience some clarity on whatever topic we have on our minds. Psychologists and counselors often recommend that we play out imagined interactions as a means to help crystallize our beliefs about ourselves or others.

One woman, Erica, shared how her father moved out when she was 14, leaving her with many unanswered questions. Now an adult and parent herself, Erica rarely hears from her dad. Despite this, she finds herself regularly imagining conversations with him, especially when faced with important decisions. "Sometimes, when I'm stressed about money or my career, I imagine asking my dad what he would do," Erica told me. "In my mind, he's calm, thoughtful, and encouraging, even though I never got to experience that from him in real life. Somehow, those imagined talks help me feel like he's still part of my journey."

This type of one-way conversation may be right for you when thinking about how you wish you could communicate with a missing or estranged parent. But you can also have imagined interactions with someone in your life when you want to practice an upcoming conversation. Thinking through the steps of communicating with your parent is a helpful processing tool and can contribute to an increased sense of well-being.

And for the daughters with a deceased parent, imagined interactions can provide an opportunity for organizing your thoughts into a cohesive conversation, curating the chaos in your mind into a cohesive interplay with your parent. The imagined interaction is a communication visualization tool that could unlock transformative thinking.

Every daughter has a "today" version of her parent, whether it be a version she can touch and feel or one that lives in her mind exclusively. Each of these is real and vital. So are the past and future versions of our parent, because they assist daughters in making decisions about how to do daughtering.

And let's not forget the many versions of you. When you notice the differences in yourself and other people over a lifespan, you create a way to conceptualize your daughtering differently. And for many of us, that's the open door that we need to feel better about the daughtering we are doing.

ACTIVITY 7: RECONCEPTUALIZING TODAY'S PARENT

This activity is intended to help you reconceptualize the parent you have today, so you can lean into the belief that your parent is a dynamic being in a state of change.

Instructions

1. Think of one parent who you will focus on to complete this activity.
2. Spend some time thinking of your parent and how they have behaved in the past. Select up to 10 words from the word bank to describe your *Yesterday Parent*. Focus on the qualities, habits, or behaviors that stood out to you.
3. Next, spend time thinking about your *Tomorrow* version. Imagine who you think (or fear) they might become in the future. Maybe you see them going down a path that makes you uneasy; or perhaps you are considering the contribution of other family members as you picture the future. Select up to 10 words from the word bank to describe this future version of your parent.
4. Next, focus on the parent you have today. Select up to 10 words from the word bank to describe your *Today Parent*. Challenge yourself to stay in the moment, even if your past or future impressions influence your thoughts.

RECONCEPTUALIZING TODAY'S PARENT WORD ASSOCIATION			
	Yesterday Parent	**Tomorrow Parent**	**Today Parent**
Word 1			
Word 2			
Word 3			
Word 4			
Word 5			
Word 6			
Word 7			
Word 8			
Word 9			
Word 10			

	Word Bank for Reconceptualizing Today's Parent
Parenting Style	adventurous, affectionate, attentive, authoritative, carefree, creative, demanding, distant, distracted, energetic, inspiring, misunderstood, nurturing, optimistic, overprotective, overwhelmed, playful, reliable, resilient, sacrificial, strict, supportive, traditional, unyielding
Health	chronically ill, declining, disabled, enduring, energetic, fatigued, fragile, healthy, immunocompromised, painful, recovering, resilient, restored, robust, stable, strong, weary
Habits	active, chaotic, disciplined, distracted, engaged, health conscious, inconsistent, mindful, overindulgent, predictable, procrastinating, repetitive, restless, routine oriented, sedentary, structured
Emotional State	angry, anxious, cheerful, content, depressed, detached, frustrated, grateful, hopeful, joyful, lonely, melancholy, peaceful, resentful, restless, serene, vulnerable
Cognition	adaptable, alert, clear headed, confused, declining, disoriented, distant, distracted, engaged, fixed, focused, forgetful, observant, perceptive, present-minded, quick thinking, sharp, sluggish, stable, unresponsive
Living Situation	accessible, assisted, comfortable, communal, constrained, crowded, familiar, independent, isolated, peaceful, remote, safe, secure, social, stressful, supportive, surrounded, temporary, transitional, uncertain
Finances	balanced, burdensome, comfortable, confident, conservative, dependent, flexible, generous, independent, insecure, predictable, resourceful, restricted, secure, spontaneous, stable, strained, tight, volatile, well planned

1. After completing the word association, reflect on what you decided:
   - What differences do you notice between the "Yesterday," "Tomorrow," and "Today" versions of your parent?
   - How does the way you view your parent today influence the way you interact with them?
   - Is there a trait or behavior in the "Today" version that surprises you or feels unfamiliar? Why?
2. Consider how these answers may guide you in your approach to your daughtering role:
   - What decisions can I make to strengthen my relationship with my parent?
   - What actions or attitudes can I adopt to embrace the "Today" version of my parent?
   - If my parent is no longer present, how can I honor or process my connection with them today?
3. Write a short affirmation or commitment to yourself about how you want to show up in your daughtering role, keeping the "Today" version of your parent in mind.

   Here's what I wrote for myself (with the help of a therapist!): *In every interaction with my mom, I want her to feel loved. I commit to speaking and responding in ways that align with this goal. When I cannot, I will allow myself to take a break and try again later.*
4. Optional: If you're comfortable, discuss your reflections with a trusted friend, sibling, or therapist. Make visible and known how you want to daughter the parent you have today.

Chapter 8

THE DIFFICULT SIDE OF DAUGHTERING

Navigating the complexities of life as a daughter is like fixing the inside of an old clock: messy and confusing. Daughters are expected to balance care, love, and connection with our parents while also minding our own needs for individuality and self-preservation. That's a hefty challenge.

This chapter is all about the tensions that arise while doing daughtering and how to best combat them. Throughout my research and interviews with women, I have heard stories of discreet, deep-seated fears (especially the fear of becoming like your mother) as well as longstanding, simmering frustrations that never seem to resolve. The key is to understand the unhealthy patterns that daughters often face and embrace the relationship tools and boundaries that foster our very best form of well-being.

As I have said throughout this book, adult daughters can redefine the role of a daughter on our own terms. But what does that look like? This chapter will dive into the unhealthy and ineffective stuff and provide recommendations for how to do things differently.

The path forward lies in engaging our family with intention, which means prioritizing resilience over rumination, dialogue over estrangement, and presence over perfection. So, think of this chapter as your permission slip to reshape the bonds in your family.

THE VERY BAD FEELINGS OF DAUGHTERHOOD

Let's just say it: Daughterhood—being a daughter—can come with some very bad, no good feelings. If that doesn't resonate with you, you're either a unicorn daughter or you're possibly a bit in denial (sorry to say!). Anger and negativity are part and parcel of showing up to interact with a parent. And too often, we fail to discuss the feeling in the pit of our stomach or the heaviness in our chests, because we feel like awful daughters—awful humans—for expressing these emotions. And these emotions can feel impossible to overcome. But I'm here to tell you the emotion we experience inside a relationship reveals the top layer of our connection, but not necessarily the root. Let's look specifically at daughters.

According to a significant body of research, adult daughters often face poorer quality relationships with their parents than do sons. These studies have found that this is because daughters are typically more invested in intergenerational relationships and have more frequent emotional support exchanges. Sometimes bad feelings occur because daughters have an overinvestment in their parents. Other times, it's guilt that arises between a daughter and her parent. Or difficulties could arise for other reasons, like an adult child living with their parent.

One reason these feelings between a daughter and her parent are particularly difficult is because they're harder to escape. Daughters with aging parents feel a social or cultural obligation, or they may be tied to their parent financially. The power differences, personality traits, and family communication patterns (or the ways that the family is used to interacting) all come into the mix to make daughtering a parent a challenging endeavor.

Bad feelings are usually the result of, not the impetus for, difficult relationships. Underneath the feelings are interactive processes at work. But conflict stemming from these emotions, when handled in unhealthy ways, can keep daughters and their parents at odds.

WHAT IS CONFLICT—AND HOW CAN YOU GET THROUGH IT?

Conflict can be defined as a struggle between two individuals who sense differing goals, perspectives, or barriers to getting their purposes met. But conflict between mothers and daughters is uniquely charged, shaped by the intimacy of the relationship and the overlapping roles of care provider, confidante, and critic. Linguist Deborah Tannen, in her book, *You're Wearing That?: Understanding Mothers and Daughters in Communication*, highlights how differing conversational styles and expectations often fuel these conflicts. Tannen explains that mothers may interpret a daughter's silence or brevity as withholding, while daughters can perceive their mom's questions as intrusive or critical. These mismatched interpretations create a cycle of miscommunication, where intentions are misunderstood and emotions flare.

But conflict, while uncomfortable, is not inherently destructive. It arises from a struggle to navigate differing goals. Expressing your needs and boundaries is a natural part of any intimate relationship. When we're close with someone, we want to be well understood and aligned in our choices and actions. But it's not possible to find that synergy 100 percent of the time. Conflict will, inevitably, arise. The challenge lies in managing conflict constructively rather than letting it fester into resentment or detachment.

Left unresolved, Tannen says, conflict can perpetuate cycles of anger, negativity, and misunderstanding, keeping both parties stuck in unproductive patterns. Two noteworthy expressions of conflict and emotion are terms you may have heard before, so I want to address those here: *Daughter rage* and *matrophobia* are expressions of anger and fear that can become debilitating if we let them take over our lives. The goal is not to allow that.

Daughter Rage

Daughter rage is a raw, usually silent, chronic emotion that stems from feelings of frustration, betrayal, or unfulfilled needs in a parent-daughter relationship. Unlike fleeting anger, daughter rage is deeply rooted and can manifest as ongoing resentment. This societal expectation to honor and respect one's parents often leaves daughters suppressing their anger, which can lead to unhealthy coping mechanisms or emotional outbursts. Many daughters struggle to articulate this rage because it feels taboo to criticize or challenge the person who gave them life.

Take Shelby's story. At age 55, she describes herself as "never not angry." Shelby told me how her whole life has been shaped by her mom Laura's compulsions. Laura has not been diagnosed with a disorder, but that's what Shelby assumes they've been dealing with: her mother has rules about where to sit, how to clean, what to touch or avoid. Looking back over her life, Shelby is resentful of her mom, describing her mom's fixations as her mom's "third child and the one she liked best." Shelby always felt as though she were in second place to an invisible force, but she was the only real human around trying to help. And now, all these years later, she's angry. She's mad at her mom for not facing and controlling her issues; she's mad at her dad for never seeking a solution or getting truly involved; she's mad at herself for having vague boundaries and overcaring for her mom since her teen years.

In Shelby's story, I see the raw contours of daughter rage. She wasn't dismissing the validity of her mom's well-being, but she was finally stepping outside of it to acknowledge the immeasurable losses that this paradigm has created for their family. This kind of rage isn't immature or selfish, it's a reclamation of a daughtering narrative that has too long been dominated by someone else's choices.

Terri Apter, in her book, *Difficult Mothers*, cuts to the heart of the issue, noting that a parent can have a powerful impact on daughters, even long after we have outgrown our dependence on them. She says a daughter's forceful, stewing anger is like a pot of water about to boil over; it didn't happen quickly. Feelings of rage can arise from persistent unmet expectations, boundary violations, as well as being dismissed and hurt. Specifically, Apter notes that when a parent treads on a daughter's individuality, it can trigger feelings of powerlessness, followed by a desire for rebellion—yes, even in adult women. This rage is not necessarily about the parent, but about the dynamics, rules, and backlash that have festered in the relationship over time. And this rage can also come from frustration with the "machine" of social expectations for daughters to prioritize family over their own needs. When a daughter tries to break out of the terrible cycle she's in with her parent, she might be shouted at, stonewalled, ostracized, or criticized. Mothers might hurt their children out of their own pain. Hurt people can hurt other people, and it's really hard for a daughter to extricate herself from painfully difficult circumstances with people she loves.

But daughters can heal from daughter rage—with plenty of compassionate self-reflection (and therapists can help!). The first step is to share the experiences you've been through. Feeling silenced, invisible, and martyred only leads to more anger. These emotions must first see the light of day before they can be resolved.

Even if open dialogue with a parent isn't an option, women can channel their emotions in other constructive ways, like sharing their story with friends, a trusted counselor, or on a social media platform. Shedding light in dark places is the first form of healing. Like sunlight bleaches garments, it can turn dark anger into something more positive. Daughter rage, when addressed thoughtfully, can become a powerful catalyst for personal growth and relational healing.

Matrophobia

Matrophobia, a term popularized by Adrienne Rich in her book *Of Woman Born*, describes the fear of becoming one's mother—a phenomenon many daughters face. The idea of "becoming my mother" can feel like a loss of individuality or autonomy, sparking anxiety and self-doubt. This fear can stem from daughters witnessing behaviors or traits in their mothers that are perceived as undesirable, oppressive, or in conflict with their own sense of self.

For some, matrophobia reflects an internalized tension between admiration for their mothers and a desperate desire to carve out a separate identity. As daughters look at their mothers, we can see what we like and dislike, encapsulated in the same being. While we may have the capacity to love our mother despite her shortcomings, we often don't think we could love ourselves with the same traits.

In a way, matrophobia demonstrates our desire to be ourselves and resist a social system that reproduces the same issues for women generation after generation. Psychologists say this tension is not merely a rejection of the mother but a reflection of daughters grappling with their own evolving identities. To achieve a separateness, the stirring inside a daughter urges her to reject her mother or the essence of becoming *like* her.

For others, matrophobia is deeply tied to cultural expectations placed and the rejection of the intergenerational transmission of these norms. The patriarchal society that holds women back is not only a "big picture" issue, but one that daughters see manifested inside their mothers individually. As their mother conforms to the expectations of a patriarchal world, a daughter who sees the strictures of these norms desires radical change. The result can be a full-form rejection of what our mothers represent: a capitulation to the pressures of patriarchal invisibility in womanhood.

Daughters often grow up observing their mothers navigate societal pressures—sacrificing personal ambitions, managing the bulk of the mental, physical, and emotional load of running a household, or conforming to rigid gender roles. The fear of repeating these patterns can create a strong resistance to identifying with their mothers, even as they inherit many of the same relational and societal challenges. After all, the invisibility of daughtering persists! Ill-equipped to tackle the social problems, women fear and scorn their mothers, creating pain for both parties.

The negative sentiment associated with matrophobia can, however, have an upside. Awareness of the fear and distaste for your mother's struggle can inspire growth and self-discovery. When we unpack the fear and find its roots—and our disgust—are with society and not our mother herself, we can begin to reframe our relationship. We can offer grace for the struggle she endured and the system that oppressed her.

We can choose, instead, to join in the fight against invisibility and societal disinterest through a powerful imagining of ourselves as a champion in our mother's name. After all, we know it's not possible to *actually* become our mothers. Rather, we must aim to reject the anchors that have held them down.

THE POWER TO CHANGE

As an adult daughter, you hold a unique power to shape your relationships—not by changing others, but by embracing your own ability to navigate conflict, set boundaries, and advocate for yourself. Relationships with parents can be deeply fulfilling if we make an effort to interact effectively. Many of us need to unlearn old patterns and find new ways of connecting, and tools like conflict resolution and boundary setting are among our best options for creating change. With a willingness to grow and try something different, you can foster stronger connections while staying true to yourself.

Practitioners agree that conflict is not only normal within close relationships, but necessary for healthy and authentic connections. When conflict arises, most of us either want to run away or have a shouting match. And while these are common responses, they're not the healthiest choices. Conflict resolution is one of the most effective paths forward. But, *sigh*, it's also very time-consuming. Avoidance or snapping are both quick solutions to problems, and they bring a level of emotional safety as we protect ourselves.

Deborah Tannen notes that the unique dynamics of the mother-daughter relationship often lead to misunderstandings, as both parties interpret words and actions through a lens shaped by deep emotional ties and expectations. While Tannen does not prescribe rigid rules, her research suggests several strategies daughters can use to foster healthier and more productive conflict resolution with their mothers:

1. **Recognize the desire for connection.** Mothers often ask questions or offer unsolicited advice as a way to maintain connection with their daughters. Rather than interpreting these actions as meddling, daughters can try to see them as invitations for dialogue. Tannen's research highlights how mothers and daughters may prioritize different conversational goals—mothers may seek connection (rapport talk), while daughters might focus on exchanging information (report talk). Daughters can bridge this gap by sharing personal experiences or emotions rather than sticking strictly to facts, fostering a more relational dialogue.

2. **Reframe criticism as caring.** Tannen notes that what daughters perceive as criticism—such as a mother commenting on their demeanor, choices, or behaviors—often stems from a place of caring. Mothers may express concern or advice because they feel responsible for their daughters' well-being. Daughters can reframe these moments by reminding themselves that their mothers are expressing love, even if the delivery feels harsh or intrusive. Daughters could try responding by acknowledging the underlying fear in their parent, saying something like "I know you're worried, but here's why I made this decision."

3. **Recognize (and avoid) conversational triggers.** Tannen points out that small comments, often meant innocuously, can escalate into conflict. She recommends that daughters pay attention to recurring triggers and, where possible, steer conversations away from those sensitive topics or reframe them in neutral terms. One way that I personally

do this is by preparing in advance of any get-togethers a list of topics that I can turn to in a quick moment. Whether it's house decorating, my kids, or a general news item, I am better able to steer a conversation to a neutral place when I am prepared in advance.

4. **Choose words that de-escalate.** When tensions arise, Tannen advises daughters to use neutral or affirming language to defuse conflict. For example, if a mother comments on a daughter's choices, instead of reacting defensively, the daughter might say, "I know you care about me, and I appreciate that." This validates the mother's intentions while steering the conversation away from conflict.

5. **Choose timing and context wisely.** Tannen notes that mother-daughter conversations are often most productive when they happen at the right time and in the right setting. Daughters should aim to address sensitive topics during calm, neutral moments rather than in the heat of frustration. Casual environments, like walks or shared activities, can also create a less pressured atmosphere for open dialogue.

6. **Focus on the relationship, not the details.** Tannen suggests that daughters should prioritize the relationship over "winning" disagreements. Instead of focusing on proving a point or correcting a mother's opinion, daughters can steer the conversation toward shared understanding and empathy. Statements like "I see where you're coming from" or "I know this is important to you" can go a long way in preserving harmony.

7. **Try active listening.** Don't forget the importance of listening without interruption or judgment. Tannen emphasizes that when we (or our conversational partners) feel heard, we are less likely to push a point or escalate the conversation. Model active listening by avoiding interruptions, nodding your head when the other person is

speaking, giving direct eye contact, and responding to what you hear.

8. **Try paraphrasing.** After a speaker is finished with their thought, try to paraphrase either the content of what they said or the emotion you observed. To review the contents of what you heard, you can say, "So, you're saying that you saw a lot of your Facebook friends posting pictures hanging out with their families?" And your parent can confirm or correct your understanding. This helps prevent confusion or distractions because you are reviewing the information right as you hear it. Another way to help someone feel heard is to respond back with the emotions you're picking up from them. For example, you can say, "I hear you saying that you felt sad about missing my baby shower." Or you can say, "It sounds like you're frustrated." These responses affirm the speaker and contribute to conversational back-and-forth. In a busy world, we are too often distracted in conversation to grasp the real meaning of what the other is conveying, but this technique can help.

9. **Point out the meta-communication.** Talking about how you talk can be a powerful tool. Daughters can say, "I feel like we're misunderstanding each other right now—can we talk about how we're approaching this conversation?" This tactic allows both parties to step back and reflect on their interaction, often defusing tension. On occasion, it's a good idea to reset the ground rules of what you find acceptable for how others are allowed to speak to you.

The strategies above, as suggested by Tannen, are a great place to start working toward effective conflict resolution with a parent. If doing all of the steps in one big sequence seems overwhelming or like some form of wishful thinking for an idyllic relationship, try instead picking just one or two strategies at first. Even when you are willing to do the hard work to improve a relationship, sometimes the other person just isn't. You may be dealing with a parent who won't be bothered to do the conversational work suggested here, or simply cannot. You can't force another person to modify their behavior. But you can learn about conflict resolution, and little by little begin to put small practices into place that can chip away at the existing family interaction patterns. I truly believe that when you change a few small things for the goal of a better relationship, you are doing such important work that will pay off in time. But, just a heads-up for some of you who have already been trying, perhaps for years unsuccessfully: it's also okay to know your limits.

HAVE THE CONVERSATION

I was speaking with Chantelle, age 44, and she told me that the biggest issue she has with her mother, Denise, is about the relationship she has with Chantelle's son, Zeb, age 17. According to Chantelle, Denise has such a close relationship with Zeb that sometimes Denise can insert herself too far into the parenting and decision-making of raising a child. Denise also talks directly to Zeb and gives him guidance, without consulting Chantelle to see if she agrees.

That seemed like a frustrating paradigm to me. Yes, Chantelle said, it is, but I don't talk to her about it. Why not, I asked? Chantelle replied that she wasn't sure why, but she just felt like it was better for Zeb to let him have his relationship with his grandma Denise. As for Chantelle, she just keeps swallowing her frustration in the name of being a good mom and good daughter.

This scenario isn't unusual. A lot of daughters have something that is preventing them from having the best possible relationship with their parent. It's like a metaphorical roadblock between them. And the daughters convince themselves it's better to just let it go, let the relationship happen as it is, and not say anything about what's bothering them.

Usually, though, there's comes a time when daughters decide to confront the roadblock, whether it's about a grandchild, money, tone of voice, or a million other possible things that bother daughters in relationship to their parents. This is not a step taken lightly, nor does it guarantee resolution. But it's a pivotal moment that requires fortitude—a willingness to face the discomfort of raw conversations and the unpredictability of their parents' responses.

As Chantelle continued to tell me her story, I could see her resolve sharpen and a new determination grow in her eyes. She said, "I think I am going to talk to my mom about this. I didn't realize how much it was bothering me until I told you about it." That's what happens with external processing. When we say things out loud, we think about them and hear them in different ways.

Organizational psychologist Karl Weick's sensemaking theory helps us understand this phenomenon. Weick said, "How do I know what I think until I see what I say?" Sensemaking theory suggests that we make meaning from our experiences when we share and discuss them with others. It's an ongoing process. I find this so helpful in explaining why I feel better rehashing a topic with my sister even if it's the fifth time we've talked it through. Sensemaking helps us decide what's plausible, and we find acceptable ways of understanding our experiences and coming to terms with events in our lives.

Marisol, a 27-year-old daughter, explained that going to her mom's house and trying to talk to her felt like walking into a courtroom. But she had resolved to talk to her mom about her feelings from her childhood. She had tried to broach the subject before and was told that she was being "dramatic." But Marisol decided she needed to get these feelings out.

She wanted her mom to know that she had often felt unsafe in her childhood. So she tried again, telling her mom about all the fear she had as a girl that was spilling over into her life today. And again, her mom dismissed her, moving around the kitchen like that conversation was over. Marisol told me that she didn't give up, determined to say what she had come to say. "I'm not saying you didn't try. I'm saying I needed something different. And I just need you to hear that."

After a long pause, her mom started talking about dinner. No apology. No big breakthrough between the two of them. But Marisol felt something shift inside her. She had spoken. She hadn't shrunk herself to keep the peace. She had stepped into the storm—and she was still standing. Whether her mom was ignoring her or simply processing, she was okay with how things went that day.

My heart sunk a little bit as I empathized with Marisol for how much it hurt her to feel a cold shoulder from her mother. But then she told me, later that night, her mom sent a text saying, "I didn't realize you felt that way. I'm thinking about what you said." It wasn't everything. But it was something. Marisol had talked about the issue she needed to get off her chest and she had seen a tiny bit of movement. She could accept that as part of the journey of transformation.

Sometimes the issue you have as a daughter isn't just between you and your parent—it involves siblings, too. Family dynamics can create unspoken alliances or invisible divides, and addressing those dynamics often means confronting siblings about their roles. These conversations can be opportunities to create understanding or establish boundaries, even if they feel tense in the moment.

Ava, age 32, is a good example. Ava had always felt like the mediator in the family. Whenever their mom made a passive-aggressive comment or stirred up drama, Ava would smooth things over. She had a younger sister, Nina, age 29, who seemed to laugh off everything their mom did or point out that what she was saying was somewhat uncouth. But when their mom's birthday dinner ended with a stand-off between Ava and her mom, Ava called Nina the following day to ask if they could talk.

Nina was reluctant to discuss the topic, but Ava persisted. "I told her, 'I get why you don't want to talk to me, but I can't keep carrying all the emotional fallout from our family alone.'" Nina told her that she assumed that Ava enjoyed being in charge and being the one to handle everything. No, Ava told her, she was tired of handling every little thing on her own. The conversation was uncomfortable—but it cracked something open. In the next few weeks and months, Ava saw Nina step up and step into conversations, even when it was uncomfortable. It wasn't perfect. But for Ava, it was a relief. Not because her sister had suddenly changed—but because she had finally stopped pretending everything was fine.

THE BLESSING OF BOUNDARIES

Boundaries are invisible guidelines that define what you will or won't allow in your interactions with others. As the saying goes, "Good fences make good neighbors." For adult daughters, boundaries are vital tools for protecting your well-being. Your well-being includes your emotional, physical, and mental health. At the same time, effective boundaries can also foster healthier family dynamics. And healthy families are what we want. With clear guidelines, you can let your loved ones know what to expect from you, while also setting the tone for what you will or won't allow in your life.

Dr. Henry Cloud, author of the well-known book *Boundaries: When to Say Yes, How to Say No to Take Control of Your Life*, says that boundaries clarify ownership: what you are responsible for and what belongs to others. A boundary is a way of saying that you take responsibility for your actions, emotions, and choices without taking on other people's junk. It's a clear way of saying what you will not accept.

Penelope, 32, for example, decided that she was unwilling to accept any more comments from her dad about her husband Pete's career choices. Pete was freelancing as a journalist working from home while caring for their twin toddler sons. Every time Penelope or Pete interacted with her dad, he asked them questions about when Pete will get a more stable job, or he'd make snarky remarks about how hard it must be for Pete to parent the two boys. Since Penelope earned enough for the family, she began to believe that these remarks were not coming from her dad's concern over finances but from his perspective on traditional household roles. One day she'd had enough and decided to set a boundary. It wasn't dramatic, but it was firm. She looked at her dad and told him she didn't want to talk about Pete's work anymore. They're not hiding anything, she said, but they're also not asking for advice. She was done being on the defensive. And she decided that her dad's discomfort was for him to manage. That's how to be healthy. It ain't easy but it's worth it.

Healthy boundaries come in many forms. Psychological boundaries protect your mental space, allowing you to engage in conversations without absorbing emotions that aren't yours. This one is especially difficult for me. These boundaries come up when families are telling stories or having discussions that veer into uneasy topics and you can feel your mood shift. Deborah Tannen offers an example of how a daughter might set a boundary while also avoiding tension. A daughter might say, "I appreciate your advice, but I feel more confident making this decision on my own." This approach validates the mother's input while asserting the daughter's autonomy.

Physical boundaries establish your comfort levels with personal space and care responsibilities. An example of enacting a physical boundary would be, if you invited everyone over for a meal and requested that it be a non-alcohol event. One of your guests shows up with a bottle of wine anyway. Your boundary is enacted by asking that person to take the bottle back out to the car. If they won't, you can ask them to leave. If they don't agree to your terms, you don't invite them to future events.

Containing boundaries, as described by Juliane Taylor Shore in *Setting Boundaries That Stick*, helps you pause before reacting, giving space for thoughtful, intentional responses. According to Shore, setting boundaries requires a clear sense of your values and the courage to enforce them. For daughters, that means knowing who you are and not letting anyone else try to change your values.

For adult daughters, this could mean learning to say no to unreasonable requests, asking for emotional space, or setting limits on time devoted to family events. Because when we're in those spaces, sometimes our containing boundaries slip. In her book, Shore leads readers through an exercise to mentally prepare for upholding our boundaries. The first step is to picture what the boundaries look like when they are in place. For me, it's like a force field, emanating from my body and surrounding me. My boundaries are an impermeable shield that is radiating powerfully from my skin. I can get close to others, but I don't have to let *their* ideas about me, *their* pain, or *their* problems in. Even within a relationship, I am still me and fully in control of what I know about myself.

If you choose to do the work of setting boundaries, you are agreeing to put yourself in a position of honor in your life. Setting and maintaining boundaries is a process of bravery and courage—the courage to say yes to your true self and what makes you feel safe, protected, valued, seen, and loved. Because you matter.

If you abandon your boundaries, you are abandoning yourself, your value system, everything you hold dear. Don't abandon yourself so that others can feel the tiniest bit better about themselves. Instead, recognize that they need to do their own work, too. And you, daughter, are not here to do everyone's work for them.

Boundaries ensure that your role as a daughter does not overshadow your identity as an individual. They are a way of saying, "I value myself, and I value our relationship enough to create healthy dynamics." Setting and maintaining boundaries allows you to protect your well-being, navigate complex family dynamics, and build authentic, fulfilling relationships.

CONNECTING WITHOUT OVERCOMMITTING

Daughters often feel it's our job to instill healthy family communication patterns, while also giving ourselves a pat on the back for the hard work it takes to make a healthy family happen. But it's not your job to turn yourself inside out and upside down for people who won't help you help them.

You might be struggling in the role you want to play as a daughter, for any number of reasons. Maybe it's time for a break and a new approach. While my interest is providing you with the healthiest tools to stay bonded to your parent and family, I want you to protect yourself as you try to stay connected, so here are some alternative strategies.

Pebbling is a light, low-pressure communication tactic used to maintain or spark connection without overwhelming either person, often through small gestures like sharing a meme, a song, or an inside joke. Inspired by penguins who gift pebbles as a symbol of nesting readiness, this approach is especially useful in emotionally complex relationships—like the kind between daughters and parents—where direct conversation might feel too intense. Pebbling allows for consistent, affectionate outreach that signals care without demanding reciprocation, creating space for connection while honoring personal boundaries. I remember telling a friend that she should try pebbling with her mom when she shared how intense every interaction was feeling. I suggested she send a short news story via text or a funny gif. It's a way to stay connected without all the intensity.

Be careful to avoid coming across as someone who is *breadcrumbing* instead, which is a negative communication pattern where you offer inconsistent attention. This is often used as a manipulative tool where you try to keep another person interested but without real intent to connect. Unlike pebbling, breadcrumbing lacks authenticity and often leads to confusion or emotional distress for the recipient. It's characterized by sporadic texts, vague plans, or fleeting social media interactions that hint at closeness but never deliver. The key difference lies in intention: Pebbling fosters genuine connection, while breadcrumbing manipulates interest without commitment.

Lastly, *grey rocking* is a strategic response to manipulative individuals, designed to make yourself appear emotionally uninteresting and neutral to stop further problems in their tracks. To use grey rocking, try responding to anything your parent says in a calm and factual way. This avoids any displays of emotion or personal disclosure that could be used against you. You can protect your energy and reduce the likelihood of escalation. This method can be particularly useful when you can't avoid a difficult person, like a coparent or grumpy grandpa, and need a way to stay present without feeding into their need for drama or control. It's not a tool for deepening relationships but it will help you survive them.

I'm not here to tell you what will work in your specific relationship, but encourage you to think outside the box; the goal is to stay in relationship with your parent while also fostering your personal well-being. Sometimes, good enough just has to be good enough.

NO CONTACT OR LOW CONTACT?

The decision to go no contact with a parent is deeply personal. A drastic choice like this is rooted in pain, frustration, or self-preservation. It's a valid concept to explore, especially when the relationship feels overwhelming and unsustainable. If you've even thought about taking this step, it's likely that the weight of the relationship simply felt too heavy to currently bear. Protecting yourself is a form of self-respect and an acknowledgment that your well-being matters.

However, from my perspective, true estrangement isn't the answer for most relationships. It may offer immediate relief, but it often leaves unresolved emotions in its wake. Relationships are rarely black-and-white, and even in difficult dynamics, there's potential for healing, understanding, or redefinition. Plus, it's my belief that there's no way to escape daughtering, even if you're not speaking to your parent. It's ingrained in your heart and mind.

I spoke with a woman who told me, "You're never no contact with your parent unless one or both of you is dead." And that's coming from someone who said she has no contact with her mother. She made the choice to limit the amount of negativity that was pouring into her life via her parent. But even after stating that preference, she still had to work to get others, like her dad, to understand the choice. He would send her letters written by her mom. Her aunts and cousins would deliver news about her mom. Even her cell phone seemed out to keep them in touch—every 90 days she had to reblock mom's phone number because she doesn't have a premium plan. So, even in the end, no contact still lets some things slip through. And she told me that she can foresee a day when she will be in communication with her mother again, though she doesn't find that idea appealing. Even so, the daughter connection persists. So I do understand that there are people in the world who are truly toxic, cruel, painful, and uncaring. And if you need to, you can avoid having contact with those individuals.

Daughtering is inherently complex, shaped by history, expectations, and emotions. Walking away entirely might seem like the only option, but with the right tools and boundaries, many relationships can be navigated in ways that honor both your autonomy and the connection you may still value. This process is nuanced, challenging, and deeply individual.

Like many daughters, you might find yourself wanting an in-between solution for how to approach being a daughter in relationship with your parent. You want to be in contact but not be beholden to your parents. Your solution could be a microdosing approach to daughtering. *Microdosing* is a term I borrow from the medical field, where you give a tiny bit of the intervention, which creates just enough of a difference to be meaningful.

Microdosing daughtering is an approach that emphasizes offering small, intentional acts of care and connection as a way of maintaining your role without overwhelming yourself. Instead of feeling obligated to manage large, time-consuming commitments, microdosing allows you to give what you can, when you can. It's a way to balance your own needs while still allowing a bit of your parent's needs to infiltrate the barrier. Daughtering doesn't always have to be a grand gesture—it can be meaningful in the smallest of moments.

Whether that's a quick, heartfelt phone call or voice note each week, sending a meme or article that resonates, or scheduling a 15-minute window to be mentally and emotionally available for listening to your parent, microdosing means approaching the labor of daughtering with measured intentionality.

The microdosing approach can take many forms: a quick text to check in, bringing some food to their house, meeting for a meal on your lunchbreak, or spending a few minutes listening to a story your parent wants to tell. These brief acts create touchpoints of connection, showing that you care without overextending yourself. For daughters juggling busy lives, microdosing can alleviate guilt while fostering a sense of consistency in the relationship. You're giving some connection to your parent but reserving your resources and private life for yourself.

Microdosing daughtering isn't about doing less but about doing what's sustainable. This approach acknowledges that relationships are built on cumulative interactions rather than isolated efforts. "It's the thought that counts," you might say. By focusing on small but sincere contributions, you can navigate the demands of daughtering with compassion—for both you and your parent.

NAVIGATING THE MOST DIFFICULT PARTS OF DAUGHTERING

As adult daughters, we navigate not just the moments of connection and care, but also the undercurrents of tension, frustration, and, at times, estrangement. Navigating negative feelings does not mean we are abandoning our daughtering role. Using tactics and strategies for daughtering aren't failure; they're self-preservation and growth. Even in difficult circumstances, we can honor ourselves while staying true to our role as a daughter. As we move forward, the goal is not to eliminate the hard parts of daughtering but to face them with awareness and intention.

Emotions like anger and negativity help to point us to larger, unresolved issues such as power imbalances, emotional manipulation, or longstanding patterns of communication breakdowns. It can often be difficult to look past these emotions in order to create effective interpersonal relationships. But that seems to be what a lot of daughters are doing. We're stuck in our feelings and trying to exist in a relationship. But we're not feeling any better on the inside and we're not moving the relationship along. We're in limbo, purgatory, or even worse, hell.

That stuck feeling is where daughters get that sense from society that we're impotent and invisible, and mere pawns in a family dynamic that we have no control over. These feelings, left unchecked, can manifest in physical symptoms like stress and fatigue or evolve into strained, disconnected relationships. Understanding the roots of anger and negativity is essential to breaking free from these cycles. Acknowledging these feelings as valid and worthy of exploration, rather than suppressing or dismissing them, can empower daughters to take the first step toward healthier interactions and self-awareness.

Beyond shaping the relationship with a parent, we as daughters also have the ability to transform ourselves. We are daughters. Full stop. All that we need to be a daughter is already inside us. If we wish to change, we can start by looking inward.

Daughtering is special because it's both who we are and what we do. It's a role rooted in identity and shaped through relationships, especially with our parents. Unlike other roles, daughtering evolves over time, offering space for reflection, care, and personal growth. It's not just about supporting others—it's also about discovering ourselves and shaping the legacy of our families with intention and heart.

ACTIVITY 8: CHECKLIST FOR HEALTHY BOUNDARIES

This checklist is a great place to start evaluating your family's boundaries. The following list contains five hallmarks—*clear communication, independence, personal space, verbal interactions,* and *expectations*—that can guide healthy interactions in families. These behaviors may be the norm for your family or they could be new ways of interacting that you'd like to see in the future. The goal of this activity is to assess what healthy and effective boundaries you currently have in place while also considering new ideas for strategies you'd like to see in the future.

Instructions: Think about recent interactions with one or more of your family members. Circle a response next to each behavior that you see within your family. Each boundary has an option for *Frequently*, *Sometimes*, and *Never*; these can be used to indicate how often you see this boundary enacted. There are no right or wrong answers. Select the best fit for each item listed by quick, gut instinct rather than deliberating a long time for an exact response.

CHECKLIST FOR HEALTHY BOUNDARIES			
Frequently	Sometimes	Never	**Clear Communication:** Open dialogue about feelings, needs, and boundaries
Frequently	Sometimes	Never	**Independence:** Individual interests and decisions are supported
Frequently	Sometimes	Never	**Personal Space:** Time and space are respected
Frequently	Sometimes	Never	**Verbal interactions:** Calm discussions; no name-calling or yelling
Frequently	Sometimes	Never	**Expectations:** Clarity on consequences for boundary violations
			Other: What are some other behaviors that you want to note?

After completing the checklist, take a moment to reflect on what the results might mean. If you have chosen *Frequently* in several of the rows above, this may indicate that you have many effective boundaries in place for your family interactions. If you selected *Sometimes* or *Never*, don't despair; everything in our families occurs in context. This is your opportunity to evaluate how your family interacts and what behaviors you might like to see more or less of in the future.

Chapter 9
THE FUTURE OF DAUGHTERING

Sweet relief. That's the feeling you can hold as a daughter who is self-aware of your role in a family and in the world. You know how much you're willing to give to this job of daughtering and you put up strong fences around the rest. You are an individual, a woman of the world, and a daughter. When you change your awareness, you change yourself. Let's go over some of the new mindsets you've gained from this book. And then we'll cover the practical steps you can implement into your life today to keep your daughtering moving forward.

LESSONS FOR DOING THE WORK

Before reading this book, you may have thought very little about your role as an adult daughter. As you incorporate the lessons from this book into a new mindset you can take forward with you, you may begin to notice a paradigm shift. Even if nothing else in your life changes, you are now more aware than ever of your importance in your family system. Let's go over some of the key takeaways that you can continue to remind yourself of as you do the work of daughtering in the days ahead.

You're Already Doing Daughtering

The first lesson is to notice and acknowledge that daughtering is a thing, and you're already doing it. Give yourself credit for that. Yes, there might still be room to evolve and try new methods. But as you think about your current level of daughtering and consider how or what to change in the future, remember that the most authentic daughtering comes from a place of wanting to grow and flourish. Effective change does not start from a place of shame or regret that you're somehow not good enough.

Shed old impressions of yourself as the wrong kind of daughter and instead embrace the notion that all daughters are daughtering the best way we possibly can. There is no one-size-fits-all approach to daughtering. The first step on the journey to being the best possible daughter you can be is to release any shame or guilt that's born from comparison. Whether it's comparison to your peers, your siblings, or even what kind of daughter your mom was to her mother, letting go of others' expectations for themselves can set you free. Because if you truly honor that all daughters can do daughtering differently and yet still be enacting the role, then you allow *yourself* the freedom to be different, too.

Daughtering Is Labor

Whether through doing, thinking, feeling, or being, the work of daughtering is happening in every facet of your heart, mind, and body. When you recognize the ways daughtering is enacted, you can also notice the resources that are pulled from you to provide daughtering for your parent. Through time, energy, mental load, or physical tasks, you are showing up for your parent and deciding to give those resources to them instead of another area of need in your life.

A lot of love labor and care provisions go unpaid in a society that views these as obligatory or even a privilege. But unpaid labor is not free. It costs someone something. And it's okay to count the cost and show others the tally; that's bringing daughtering out of the shadows.

Daughtering Is Invisible

Due to complex cultural and familial circumstances, the nature of daughtering is often ignored, uncalculated, and therefore invisible. Without the specific language to describe what you're doing as a daughter, it can be difficult to describe to others the impact of your role. But daughtering is no less real because it's invisible (isn't music pretty darn real?).

The invisibility of various experiences happens because society doesn't take notice or shine a light on the topic. You might even be using borrowed language like "best friends" or "mothering my mother" to try and describe your journey through adult daughtering, yet you can see how woefully inadequate these terms are.

But, as a society, we are also great at embracing neologisms (new words) that help explain previously ineffable experiences. And when we talk about our stories, the conversation and consequently the language can grow. We have a responsibility to our whole community of daughters to do our part by using the right words for our role and work—because the work of daughtering matters.

Daughters Have the Agency to Change

You have the agency as a woman and a daughter to do things differently. The benefit of changing your daughtering is not just for you, but also for those who are watching you (your nieces, your children, your friends' kids, and even your extended network and online friends). You can create a new paradigm for future generations about what daughtering is supposed to look like by rejecting the status quo and embracing a new kind of daughtering.

The changes you make can contribute to the freedom of the next generation to do daughtering in a healthy, effective way that prioritizes the autonomy of the women doing it. Think of yourself as a steward of a role, and you can be a crucial part of solidifying this dynamic of good daughtering. Your work today can make it easier to do daughtering in the future, more accessible to discuss and embrace the different forms of daughtering and ultimately remove barriers for daughters coming after you.

Daughtering Is Inclusive and Flexible

Daughtering as a role is big enough and broad enough for all who attempt it—just like the definition of family. There are a lot of structural forms that we consider to be family systems, and whether or not these apply to you or someone you've met, they apply to millions of other people. One of the productive mindsets you can embrace as a daughter is to stay loose with family forms and what they mean to others. Like many things in our world, families are a social construct, and they mean what we allow them to mean.

In the same way, research is still catching up with the question about who gets to do daughtering, as it relates to gender and sexuality. Daughtering can be a bit sticky if you think about it as a role that applies only to women. But what is a woman? And how does daughtering apply for those who are gender-nonconforming?

The truth is that we don't know how gendered expectations and language will continue to change, but again, we can be loose with the idea of daughtering and apply the term as an ally would. When I think of the best possible future for spreading the love of doing daughtering, I foresee a broad-spectrum adoption of the usage and ideology of daughtering. If sharing it with all those who are gender-variant helps achieve that goal, then it seems worthwhile to share the moniker of daughter with all who will claim it. The key to embracing daughtering as a phenomenon is allowing it to change over time.

The Only Constant Is Change

Daughtering will continue to change over your lifespan. Your age and circumstances as well as your parents' aging will create a revolving door of opportunities to try daughtering in new ways.

This state of flux necessitates a mindset of assessment and adaptation for your daughtering. Rather than assuming static interplay, you can imagine a dynamic, evolving relationship that deserves to have an up-to-the-moment approach. A pattern or boundary that used to work for you may not be successful for all time.

Remember to occasionally pause and reflect on your daughter role so you can calibrate the level of involvement and intensity that is *needed* and whether you have the resources to *meet that need*. Thinking about our thinking—or thinking about our behavior—is a metacommunication strategy that allows us to get outside of ourselves and view our lives from a broader context.

A daughter who can assess herself, her parent, and the context of both lives in the moment can then adapt with realistic optimism. The clarity of who you are dealing with will allow you to best manage your resources effectively.

Managing Resources Is Essential

Your resources are limited. Effective daughtering means managing them wisely. Just as parents hire a babysitter to go out on date night, you can consider how to outsource your daughtering, too. You can rely on siblings, aunts, uncles, grandkids, friends, neighbors, and the rest of the community to take some of the load of your parents' needs. It doesn't have to be all on you.

When you recognize the daughtering you are doing and the resources you are allocating to the role, the next step is to effectively manage those resources. Your finances, time, energy, and mental space are finite. Your parents are key figures in your life, but their needs are not a priority above everything else, all the time. Instead, you can pick and choose how and when to engage. You can lean into your strengths as a daughter to decide how best to show up for your parent.

Daughter with Your Strengths

Consider your strengths as a daughter. Are you good at listening? Best at making something fun? Quick to respond on the family group chat? Focus on these skills and the virtues that you bring to your daughtering role within a family. You can promote your own happiness and increase the relational satisfaction of others by applying your strengths and skills within your family. The added benefit of focusing on the positive is that there's less time and energy to dwell on the negative or difficult aspects that often accompany family life.

Daughters can avoid resentment and rumination—both killers of personal happiness and lifelong contentment, according to research—by focusing on things you do well. Remember, promoting your personal wellness is a choice. That choice also benefits those around you, creating a cycle of connection and reinforcing positivity. Long-term connection—that daughters specialize in building—can stave off loneliness and enhance mental and physical health for all family members involved.

In a way, applying your strengths in a family relationship is like putting a salve on a wound. Daughters, I'd like to think we have this magical family healing property available to us if we access it for the benefit of all involved. I envision a bright future worldwide if we can calculate, calibrate, and change our daughtering for good. There's an activity at the end of this book where you can engage in community building through a daughter lens.

One way to lean into our strengths and focus on positivity is by applying a framework for *new* situations as they arise. Brené Brown wrote about a tool that she uses to assess situations when they come up and she is tempted to be annoyed or frustrated instead of empathetic and understanding. She said she tries to pause and use the "Hypothesis of Generosity" to assess a situation. She suggests asking, "What's the most generous interpretation I can have for what happened in that situation?" This question promotes extending grace to others who might be stuck in sticky circumstances.

For example, if I hear that my dad and aunt got into an argument, rather than jumping to my dad's defense and sending off a quick string of angry texts to my auntie, I can pause and apply the Hypothesis of Generosity. Maybe my aunt was having a bad day. Maybe my dad interpreted her texts poorly. Or maybe there's some other information that I don't have. Pausing to think generously can help inform my next steps as a daughter.

While I want to support my dad, I also want to create family harmony more generally, because I know the ripple effect negativity can have. Rather than defaulting to negative or pessimistic views, practicing the Hypothesis of Generosity helps reframe interactions with compassion. And it allows us to consider that people's actions may stem from struggles we cannot see, fostering empathy and reducing conflict in our relationships.

Creating a Legacy

A legacy is created as others watch and learn from you. But it can also be built actively as we teach and ask others to view us. A legacy is not only about how we are remembered, but how we shape the future.

A thoughtful exercise to engage in is consideration of how we *teach* daughtering. We all learned our daughtering somewhere, from someone, most likely passively from seeing our moms and grandmothers, watching television and movies, and talking to friends. But as we envision a new future where daughtering is visible and well understood, we can begin to frame how we want to shape the future of daughtering. What will you teach your daughter? What will you teach your nieces and neighbor kids about their worth as a daughter? What daughtering identity do you want others to notice when they think of you?

You can even teach and train daughtering in your church or temple when you volunteer to work with children and demonstrate how to behave around elders. In addition to thinking of *who* to influence, we can be intentional purveyors of daughtering efforts through our mindful approach about *how* to do daughtering.

My suggestion for anyone interested in training others is to first do the work yourself. You can start with the activities provided in this book. Then, you can begin to create a paradigm from which to operate your platform of development in daughtering.

If, throughout adolescence, women are instructed, advised, corrected, and are witness to a form of proactive daughtering in the women around them, the rising women in our world can mindfully approach the practice of engaging with their families. Instead of *reacting* to contexts and situations within families, today's and tomorrow's daughters can take a proactive, strengths-based approach to forming the kinds of relationships they long for.

WHAT'S NEXT? STEPS TO APPLY IN YOUR EVERYDAY LIFE

With our mindsets on daughtering percolating and calibrating, we can think about starting some simple everyday practices for effective daughtering.

Be an Advocate for Daughters

Each of us carries a role in supporting the vision of a future where daughtering is visible and valued. Tell yourself often that you are a good daughter, doing hard work, and deserve to be recognized. Remember that even if you can't change others, you can change yourself from the inside out. This starts with expressing gratitude (from you to yourself) for the daughtering you've done in the past and are doing now.

One way to remind yourself of the importance of your daughtering is by repeating a mantra. You might say something like "I'm doing the work of daughtering and because of me, the family is held together. Thanks, me." Another phrase that could help overworked daughters is "I deserve to put myself first and the family will still be bonded if I take a little break." Work on a mantra that best suits your situation.

Your next best asset in the push for advocacy and a revamped view of daughtering is your family. Remember, these people like you and trust you, which means they're more likely to be swayed by your persuasive appeals and explanations about how important daughtering is (for you and them).

When you decide to have a conversation with your parent, remember to pick your moment wisely. You can even bring up daughtering before, during, and after big events like weddings, funerals, and graduations—yep, I did just say that. These are your opportunities to point out specific tasks and responsibilities that you took on as a daughter for the sake of others. This part can get a little bit tricky, because some prickly people may take your comments as whining or complaining and try to give you a hard time. If they respond by saying that they work too or everybody's already doing that (or something even more condescending), remember to keep it cool and pleasant. Say yes, directly and calmly. Yes, you see other people are doing daughtering and yes, we'd all like appreciation for it.

The real purpose of these conversations is to get the work of daughtering on record. The more your family is able to recognize daughtering when they see it, the more they will see it without prompting, and this is the process that creates meaningful mattering.

Lastly, in these conversations you can seize the opportunity to frame the future. No matter what things are like now, there's always room for growth, transformation, and change. You can use future-oriented discussions to redefine family dynamics and mutual responsibilities. That looks like talking about how you want the *next* holiday to go or what you envision for the upcoming graduation. It means projecting a picture for what interactions, get-togethers, phone calls, texts, and visits *could look like* if the family works together in their roles to create bonding moments. You can use your words to create a new reality where daughtering is noticed and appreciated.

Set Boundaries for Healthy Daughtering

Daughters can avoid resentment and burnout by setting up strong boundaries for your time and energy. Nobody else can do this for you. You have to value yourself enough to put up the metaphorical fences that protect your life. When you face a heavy emotional task, like "I need to call my mom tonight because she's going through something and I'm the only one she can talk to," remember that your mom is a full human being with lots of options to find friends, community, and a partner. You are not required to be all things to all people. It's also important to remember that enacting boundaries can be awkward and frustrating at first, but the value-add is worth it in the long run.

Anticipate Your Changing Daughtering Needs

To be most effective as a daughter, you can actively begin to anticipate the adjustments coming to your daughtering in the future. Specifically, you can start thinking about the eldercare needs of your parent and the time when you will be called upon to support them through death and dying.

Senescence is the term for the period in an adult's life when physical and mental health begin a natural decline. Science does not provide us with a specific age that is as easy to pinpoint as when children go through adolescence, but senescence can be observed in adults as the physical and cognitive abilities change and regress little by little, year over year. Some might say, we're all in the process of dying every day. Though we cannot pinpoint this milestone by age alone, you will recognize this happening as your parents start needing more love, care, and consideration, though they likely still remain independent and relatively healthy. The challenge for daughters is to recognize the kinship shift—discussed previously, this is a term that describes the changing nature of our relationship with our parents as they age—that we see in our parents and address their changing cognition and physical abilities.

If you and your parent are approaching this life phase, you can create mental and emotional space for processing all that comes with the end of your parent's lifetime. Namely, you can spend time thinking about and discussing your parent's death and dying expectations. In some families, conversations about someone's wishes for their death and dying might come easily. Just the other day, my son sent me a text message that read, "When you die, I'm going to turn you into a tree." And he sent a picture of a man sitting under a big oak tree. I loved it. That's exactly how I want my remains to be cared for and he knows it because we've discussed it openly.

On the other hand, my mother-in-law hates any discussion that has to do with medicine, hospitals, illness, death, funerals, wills, or the stuff she will leave behind. So, we tread much more carefully with her when these topics come up. As someone in her late 70s, she's earned the right to determine how we discuss age-related concerns and dying. Whereas my own mom, who is also in her 70s, has already picked out her funeral songs and likes to sing them to me on the phone.

For those who find it challenging to discuss death and dying, but also know it is an acute need, consider the idea of family storytelling about the past as a way to think about the future. Family stories provide lessons and insights about how previous generations of our family interacted and behaved. These stories help us understand how "our people" do family, make choices, and live our lives according to family roles. As stories are told and retold, the narrative inheritance we gain is a sense of who we are within that family. These tellings and retellings are not static, but change, have layers, and new meanings are uncovered.

Rather than asking your mother what she might want for her own death, discussions about how others within your family have experienced elderhood, death, and dying in the past can reveal someone's point of view and perspective on these important topics. This is the kind of requesting and receiving that is an essential feature of daughtering with intentionality.

In practice, this looks like talking about your aunt's death from 10 years ago and discussing what went well and what could have changed in the time period leading up to her becoming sick, dying, her funeral, legal stuff with the estate, and more. Daughters and their parents can talk about family mottos, like the one my family holds, which is "To be is better than to seem." Sharing this with family members and embracing it as a mantra connects me anew to my maternal lineage.

For parents who are looking to help their daughters during this stage of life, there are options. One practice, popularized by Scandinavian author Margareta Magnusson in her book *The Gentle Art of Swedish Death Cleaning*, suggests individuals give away, sell, or throw out the extra possessions they no longer need in order to make things simpler for the individuals who will survive them. And if your family really gets into these pre-elderhood preparations, there's always interesting (and important) conversations to be had about finances and family secrets, too.

Tell Your Daughtering Story Online

Not only is sharing your story a great way to celebrate and shout out the details of doing daughtering, but it's also an effective processing tool for those who need help and healing. And it can be a form of advocacy. If you struggle to find individuals in your family or friend group who want to intellectualize and analyze the role of daughtering with you, rest assured that your new friend group is waiting for you online. As shared in many stories throughout the pages of this book, social media platforms and other places to write your story are widely available. Additionally, writing out your thoughts can be more than a trivial exercise; it can potentially unlock real healing. Be sure to create a family hashtag and also tag me in the post. I want to see your stories!

Use Technology to Connect

Today's modern technology goes way beyond social media platforms. There are options to lean into modern advancements even if you never want to be on social media. You can enhance your daughtering within your family and peer group by using your phone or device to do daughtering in community. Technology helps make the work more efficient and conducive to your lifestyle. Communication technologies are becoming richer—meaning they offer better sound, image, and overall quality without glitches—which can reduce the need to communicate live, in person, or face-to-face to achieve daughtering that satisfies your parent. You can please your loved ones while using your resources effectively.

One way that women can connect with their family members in a way that is easy is through gifs and memes. Gifs are moving images that you can find in the "images" section of your text message app. Memes are funny images, videos, or text that share bits of culture and are sent to others to make them laugh or think about something new. Sending a gif or meme allows you to show care and "show up" in the relationship, while also avoiding a discussion that's weighty or might cause conflict. Try placing these free add-ons into your text, chat, or email conversations to get a boost of frequency in your messaging, while preserving your sanity. The best part is that you don't need to come up with something original; the whole point of these little funnies is to *not* reinvent the wheel, but to share something that is very repeatable.

Another great way to leverage technology as a daughter is through video calls. A video call can enhance an interaction without a lot of added effort. One benefit of a video call is that it can help your conversational partner to be more present and less distracted because they're using both sound and visuals to chat. Another bonus is that you can use whatever's in the background of your settings to come up with topics, reducing the need to get into tense conversations on topics you don't want to talk about. Technology can help both with quality and quantity when trying to connect with loved ones.

Get creative with technology when thinking about how to increase volume of communication connections. A digital photo frame, for example, lets you share updated images from an app if you're out of the state or the country. Whether you are trying to protect your images from the broader internet or interacting with a loved one who doesn't use technology very effectively, frames like this one can bridge the divide.

Using technology to get more efficient at daughtering means you have conserved time and energy for other things. Of course, technology comes at a price. If you can afford it, get it, even if it means you're the one paying for someone else in the family to have access (new phone, Wi-Fi bill, etc.). Is it fair that you are always the one paying? No, it's not fair, but it's a good use of the money if you can leverage your financial resources to help you do daughtering more smoothly.

Let AI Help You Find Your "Voice"

This last tip is a bit of a hybrid, both digital and analog. If you have a family member who cannot (or will not) participate in the modern technologies described above, try sending a letter or card for special occasions.

Not a poet? You can use technology to help you write your message with the help of AI tools like ChatGPT or Microsoft Copilot. Here's how it works. You will write a description and prompt into the AI platform, then receive an output. Continue to tweak your request in a back-and-forth chat style communication with the AI tool until you receive something that is just right for your use.

Try constructing your prompt using these ideas on a site like chatgpt.com: Describe yourself and your relationship with your parent. Perhaps provide a past writing sample if you really want it to have your voice (language that sounds like you). Provide details about what kind of message you want, including length and tone, humor, or specific topics. If the response from ChatGPT is not quite right, you can respond by asking for something shorter, funnier, warmer, or that sounds like a 90s pop star wrote it. Whatever your heart's desire, you can add that to your prompt.

Over time, an AI tool can learn your preferred language, voice, humor, audience, and more. Be sure to create an account so your missives are saved for the future. Tricks like this can help you reduce the time, effort, and emotional strain of coming up with a message from a blank page (or buying a greeting card from the drugstore). Don't feel bad about asking for some assistance from your AI helper and then signing your name to it. This did indeed come from your brain and your heart, but with some help with the words from artificial intelligence.

Build New Daughtering Traditions

Today is a good day to start something new and put it on the family calendar for the upcoming year. Want a family trip to Alaska? Or need everyone to pitch in for a round-robin dinner at the next Hannukah celebration? The options are endless for how to join together with family. Each time you do something new, it's an opportunity to state that this is now a tradition.

Traditions are meant to be repeated, so you are creating the impetus for more merriment in the future, all centered around you and your contributions to the family. Give it a try, even if the new tradition or celebration is small. Every little bit of recognition for your daughtering is important and meaningful.

Apply a Positive Mindset to Your Daughtering

You can find meaning wherever you look for it when you apply a positive mindset. I encourage you to put this last recommendation into place as soon as possible. You can try focusing on the good, the positive, and the valuable parts of being a daughter. To do this, you must apply mindful attention to the thoughts and words you are using when describing your daughtering role. If you notice negativity, now is the time to turn it around.

One way for you to focus on the good in families is to do some positive thinking. If you've never done this before, you may be skeptical that thinking work can change anything in your life. But research has shown that thinking through a past event in a new way can offer different interpretations and new emotions about it as well. This process is called intentional meaning making.

According to psychologist Crystal Park's meaning-making model, this strategy involves actively reinterpreting past experiences by aligning their initial meaning with a broader global meaning rooted in our core beliefs, goals, and sense of purpose. Put more simply, we think of a past event and then ask ourselves questions, like "What big world event was that related to?" or "How did something like that help shape who I am today?" This intentional reframing can create a more compassionate and wise understanding of difficult experiences. You can use intentional meaning making to reinterpret significant life events and calibrate what they mean to you now as an older, wiser daughter.

I have done this contemplative practice myself to get a gut check on whether I was holding on to old hurt and pain when I didn't need to. Revising your interpretation of the past is a conscious choice, but it doesn't mean forgetting or moving on. Nobody is saying that this type of process instantly heals something in you and that you will forever shed the experience. Instead, this process of intentional meaning making is about transforming your perspective by integrating past events into a more coherent life story.

This reinterpretation helps reduce emotional distress and fosters resilience, allowing for personal growth despite past challenges. If it sounds too big and hairy to achieve on your own, consider asking a trained professional to walk through this process with you. Be careful about asking a peer or family member who might unintentionally touch on something tender that needs a professional's care.

CONCLUSION

Daughtering is not about perfection or endless sacrifice—it's about recognizing your worth, your boundaries, and the real contributions you make in your family and the world. You've taken a journey through the hidden labor of daughtering, named the invisible burdens, and explored ways to reclaim your energy and reshape your relationships. You've learned that feeling like the wrong kind of daughter isn't a personal failing—it's the result of outdated expectations and unspoken cultural norms that place heavy, unseen demands on daughters. But you are enough. You are the right kind of daughter for right now.

By becoming aware of these dynamics, you've begun rewriting the story. You've seen how advocacy, communication, and boundary setting can create more balanced, healthier relationships. You've understood that asking for help isn't weakness—it's wisdom. Through this journey, you've shifted from feeling stuck or unseen to embracing your role with clarity and intention.

The future of daughtering isn't about doing more, it's about doing daughtering differently. It's about making room for joy, ease, and pride in the relationships you choose to nurture. It's about legacy building with intention, fueled by self-awareness and mutual respect. You are already equipped with the tools to create better connections—not just with your family, but with yourself.

As you move forward, hold on to the knowledge that you matter, that you are capable of redefining what it means to be a daughter on your own terms. Relief comes not from achieving some idealized version of a daughter, but from realizing you've already been doing the work, even when no one noticed. Now, you notice. And that changes everything.

ACTIVITY 9: SCRIPT FOR A DAUGHTER-TALK

This activity helps you prepare for a meaningful and direct conversation with your parent(s) about your responsibilities or other concerns in your relationship. Use the prompts below to guide your thoughts and create a personalized script for the conversation.

Step 1: Set the Tone

Start off by describing your relational connection. This can create a positive environment that will foster the rest of the conversation. Remember, don't try to be too syrupy sweet if that's not your typical manner of speaking. Be authentic to yourself.

Questions for you to consider:

- How do you want to greet your parent(s) to set an open and positive tone?
- If not overtly positive, how can you set up a neutral space for talking?
- Example of setting the tone to start the conversation: *"Hi Mom, I wanted to talk with you about something important because I care about our relationship."*

- **Write your opening line.** Your opening line:

  ....

  ....

  ....

Step 2: Explain Your Intention

Let your parent(s) know why this conversation matters and what you hope to achieve. Describe the main topic. This will create clarity around the need for the conversation.

Questions for you to consider:

- What is the "thing" you're here to talk about?
- Why is it important to talk about this now?
- What do you hope the conversation will accomplish for both of you?
- Example of framing the main topic of conversation: *"I want us to be on the same page about the reasons I am changing my job. Let's talk about what I can realistically do for this family with this new responsibility."*
- **Write your intention.** Your intention:

  ....

  ....

  ....

Step 3: Share Both Your Feelings and Observations

Describe your emotions and observations about your role as a daughter. Try using "I" statements that describe your perspective without placing blame.

Questions for you to consider:

- How have you been feeling about your responsibilities as a daughter?
- What specific examples or situations illustrate your feelings?

- Example of your feelings/observations: *"Lately, I've been feeling a bit overwhelmed by everything I'm doing, like handling errands and acting as a peacemaker for you and Aunt Sue."*
- **Write your observations. Your observations:**

....

....

....

Step 4: Invite Collaboration

Ask for their thoughts and feelings to create a two-way conversation.

Questions for you to consider:

- What would you like to ask your parent(s) in order to better understand their perspective?
- How can you show that you value their input?
- Example of collaboration: *"What do you think about what I'm saying? Anything to add that can create some perspective for me? Are there things you'd like to see done differently?"*
- **Write your questions. Your questions:**

....

....

....

Step 5: Suggest a Way Forward

Offer a possible plan to your parents and allow their input.

Questions for you to consider:

- What are some ideas you have for addressing the concerns you've shared?
- How can you involve your parent(s) in creating a plan that works for both of you?

- Example of a suggestion: *"One idea I had is setting specific days for our calls so we both have more predictability. Does that sound helpful?"*
- **Write your suggestions. Your suggestions:**

....

....

....

Step 6: End Strategically

Conclude the conversation with gratitude.

Questions for you to consider:

- How do you want to thank your parent(s) for listening or participating in the conversation?
- What feelings or hopes do you want to express as you end the talk? Try to avoid restating problems or devolving into negativity.
- Example of closing line: *"Thank you for talking this through with me. I want to keep working on it together."*
- **Write your closing. Your closing:**

....

....

....

Tips for Writing Your Script

- Keep your language clear and respectful.
- Use specific examples to make your points relatable.
- Be patient with yourself and your parent(s) as you navigate the conversation.
- If the conversation feels challenging, remind yourself that the goal is mutual understanding, not perfection.

ADDITIONAL ACTIVITIES

As you reach the end of this book, your daughtering journey is just beginning. The following bonus activities are designed to help you continue reflecting, growing, and taking meaningful action in your role as an adult daughter. Use them as tools to deepen your insight, challenge old patterns, and move forward with purpose. Effective daughtering is at your fingertips.

ACTIVITY 10: DAUGHTERING HAPPINESS CHECKLIST

In your role as a daughter, you experience happiness in different ways. Some activities bring immediate joy and comfort, while others provide deeper meaning and long-term satisfaction. Use this checklist to reflect on what brings you hedonic (pleasure-based) and eudaemonic (meaning-based) happiness so you can begin to become aware of the potential downsides of each.

Check off what applies to your experience and add your own examples.

Hedonic Happiness: Joy and Pleasure in the Moment
- Spending time with your parent(s) doing fun activities (e.g., watching TV together, going out for a meal)
  Downside: Can be fleeting and may not always lead to deeper connection.
- Receiving compliments or appreciation for your efforts (e.g., "Thanks for helping out today.")
  Downside: Might feel hollow or focused on the wrong aspects for which you were wanting gratitude.
- Enjoying casual, lighthearted conversations (e.g., reminiscing about old memories or sharing jokes)
  Downside: Might avoid discussing important or difficult topics.
- Being pampered or cared for by your parent (e.g., being cooked for, getting gifts)
  Downside: Creates imbalance in the relationship or continues power balance from childhood.
- **Other:**

....
....
....
....

Downside:

....
....
....
....

Eudaemonic Happiness: Meaning and Purpose for a Lifetime
- Providing care for your parent in times of need (e.g., helping them through a crisis or transition)
  Downside: Can be emotionally draining and time-consuming.

- Offering emotional support during tough conversations (e.g., discussing family issues or life challenges)
Downside: Might lead to conflict or require heavy emotional labor.
- Participating in long-term planning or decision-making (e.g., managing finances, planning for the future)
Downside: Can feel overwhelming and create tension over differing opinions.
- Helping maintain family traditions or values (e.g., organizing family gatherings, retelling stories)
Downside: May lead to pressure or a burdening sense of obligation.
- **Other:**

....

....

....

....

Downside:

....

....

....

....

Reflection: What kind of pleasure or happiness are you finding in doing daughtering? Is it balanced or skewed? Are you an "enjoy today" or "do it for tomorrow" kind of daughter? Once you've learned about your hedonic and eudaemonic happiness opportunities as a daughter, you can begin to calibrate where you want to put more (or less) attention. If you see a lot of short-term, fun things, but long for a satisfying, lifelong, purpose-driven life, then add more activities in the eudaemonic category. The goal of this checklist is to help you see where you are putting your daughtering energy and what you get out of it, even if it's not immediately obvious as a form of happiness.

ACTIVITY 11: WRITING YOUR DAUGHTERING MISSION STATEMENT

A Daughtering Mission Statement is a personal declaration of how you wish to honor your role as a daughter, continue your relationship with your parent(s), siblings, and extended family, reflect your values and goals, while contributing to the collective daughterhood of women doing daughtering.

Find a quiet place to work. Take a few minutes to reflect on your role as a daughter, considering cultural and modern influences. Think of your relationship with your parent(s), sibling(s), or the other people and groups with whom you do daughtering. Consider how you envision your daughtering role evolving over time. Write out any thoughts you have for the prompts below or simply hold the thoughts and ideas quietly inside you.

Thought Prompts
- **Values:** What core values guide your daughtering role? (values such as: honesty, tolerance, compassion, boundaries)
- **Culture:** What are the cultural influences that are important to your personal and collective story? Do you claim ancient knowledge from your motherline?
- **Legacy:** What do you hope to carry forward from your family's story? Is there anything you want to do differently?
- **Balance:** How can you integrate care for your parent(s) into your own care and well-being?
- **Impact:** What kind of impact do you want to have in your relationship with your parent(s)?
- **Beliefs:** How do you want parents or others to feel when they think of you as a daughter?

Use insights from your reflective thinking above, create a draft of your mission statement, which can be a sentence or even a paragraph. You could start with phrases like "As a daughter, I strive to . . ." or "My mission is to . . ." or even "I am committed to . . .". Add in your values, actions, and impact. Include specifics related to your family traditions and what you look forward to seeing improved. Be sure to include your own well-being in the mix.

Framework:

"My mission as a daughter is to [*your core value*] by [*specific actions or behaviors*] so that [*the impact you hope to have*]. I will honor [*family tradition, value, or lesson*] while creating space for [*what you wish to change or improve*]. In balancing my role as a daughter with my other priorities, I will [*how you plan to maintain personal well-being*]."

Example:

"My mission as a daughter is to be present with my parent by communicating supportive comments and sometimes remaining silent. I want my mom to feel appreciated and understood, knowing that I love her—I even like her—and she's a good mom. I aim to carry forward the value of family loyalty while breaking the cycle of emotional burnout by setting healthy boundaries. In balancing my role as a daughter, I will regularly take time away from events that stress me out and choose to be honest when I need to share something important."

After reading over your Daughtering Mission Statement (or a few different drafts), ask yourself if it rings true to you and your ethos. Does it honor your personal goals while also incorporating your parent(s) as fully as possible? Have you incorporated both eudaemonic and hedonic elements that honor your lifetime happiness and the momentary flashes of joy? Revise if necessary, adding more specific details and actions that fit your daughtering style.

And if you're comfortable doing so, share your Daughtering Mission Statement. Write it on a sticky note and place it on your mirror. Text it to a friend or family member. Make a social media post about it and invite others to share their thoughts with you.

ACTIVITY 12: COMMUNITY CHANGE

In this activity, you can explore the ways adult daughters shape and influence their communities by drawing on the values, skills, and perspectives developed through their experiences. This activity is designed to help you think about social, legal, and cultural changes that could support daughters and families more effectively.

Directions
1. **Identify a community impact area.**
   - Consider an area where you'd like to see change that could benefit daughters and families. This could be a new law, a workplace policy, or even a federal holiday. Ask yourself, "What would make the lives of daughters (and those they care for) better or more supported?"
2. **Answer the following questions.**
   - What is one new law, workplace policy, or federal holiday you'd like to see created?
   - How would this change benefit daughters specifically?
   - What are some steps you can take to advocate for this change?
3. **List your personal action goals.**
   - Write down a short, specific goal for yourself. This could be as simple as having a conversation with friends about the idea, joining a local organization, or researching policies to get a better understanding of what needs to change.
4. **Action-reflection.**
   - After thinking through how to be an agent of change, reflect on how pushback as a daughter helps build confidence in your ability to shape your community and influence social change. Have you ever thought of yourself as a vehicle for social change?

ACTIVITY 13: IF I COULD WAVE A MAGIC WAND

Imagine that you are holding a magic wand and with one wave, you can reshape your family dynamics, redefine your daughtering role, and create a world where supportive, loving relationships are effortless and mutually fulfilling. Yes, it's a *very* magical wand. In this future, anything is possible—relationships are exactly how you wish them to be, with no societal constraints, time pressures, or financial worries. Don't worry about being realistic, feasible, or sensible. Dream big. Let the magic in. Follow the steps below to envision a future with a magical difference.

Step 1: Visualize the Ideal Future

Take a deep breath, close your eyes, and picture a future where daughtering works perfectly for you and your loved ones. Reflect on:

- How you feel when engaging with your family.
- How your relationships function, including respect, boundaries, and shared care.
- What support looks like from your family, community, and broader society.

Step 2: Dream Big

Answer the following prompts (out loud or on paper) as if there are no limits—be creative and bold:

1. Communication:
   - If communication were effortless, how would you and your loved ones connect?
   - What tools, methods, or rituals would make staying connected joyful and easy?
2. Support and Care:
   - How would caregiving and support happen in your ideal world?

- Who would be involved, and how would responsibilities be shared?
3. Celebrations:
   - How would your role as a daughter be celebrated and recognized?
   - What are the wins that would be noticed and cherished by others?
4. Societal Impact:
   - If society fully understood the value of daughtering, what cultural norms, workplace policies, or government programs would exist?
   - What would your friends say about being a daughter in the world today?
5. Personal Fulfillment:
   - How would you balance your daughtering role with personal growth, rest, and joy?
   - What legacy would you want to build through your relationships?

Step 3: Make It Personal

What's one more thing that you would absolutely *LOVE* to see happen? This may be something so important, enormous, or impactful that it's *almost too big* to wish for. Push yourself to admit the thing that you really want most in your relationships.

Step 4: Take Action

Look at your responses. Even in today's very imperfect world with very imperfect people, is there one thing you do or try to make the world a little more magical?

ACKNOWLEDGMENTS

I am sending out a big thanks to Karen Murgolo, my literary agent at Aevitas Creative Management. Not only did you find me and my research, but you encouraged me to write a book that women need. And you've been so patient teaching me everything about the new world of publishing. You've wrestled with me over the best possible material and represented my interests in the kindest way. Thank you to the rest of the team at Aevitas, including Todd Shuster and David Kuhn, for working so hard to get this book sent around the world.

Likewise, I am so grateful to my editor, Libby Burton, at Dey Street Books. You lived and breathed this material with me; you let the message transform you; you have nurtured and protected this book in a way that I am so grateful for and comforted by. Thanks also to Chelsea Herrera, who not only worked on this book but kept us organized and timely. Thank you to Anna Montague, who was among the first to believe in what this book could be. And a huge amount of gratitude to Carrie Thornton, who has believed in the necessity of a book on daughtering from the earliest days. I am so grateful for your support and belief in me and my work. A special thanks to the marketing and publicity teams, especially Allison Carney, Kasey Feather, and Heidi Richter at HarperCollins and Morrow Group, who have spent time and energy bringing this book to every shop and customer who needs a little oomph in their life.

Next, I send my sincere thanks to the busy women who are smart and funny and thoughtful and gave their time to reading drafts of this book and providing feedback. Readers Karen, Kaitlin, Michelle, and Janiece, I appreciate this gift so much and want you to know how meaningful it was to me that you said yes to being a reader and gave your attention to this goal.

I couldn't have brought you these ideas without the stories from the women who are living daughtering right now and shared their lives with me. Thank you to all the participants of my research studies who have opened themselves up, authentically and vulnerably, to tell me what it's like being an adult daughter in the world today.

Next, I want to say thank you to the teachers who meaningfully impacted my education and told me that I was good enough and smart enough to be a professor and a writer. From San Antonio, Texas, I thank Mrs. Ramos (first grade, when I won the spelling bee), Mrs. Pelham (second grade, who let me read MLK's "I Have a Dream" speech to the whole school over the loudspeaker), Mrs. Kelly (fourth grade, who helped me with self-control), Mrs. Recker (fifth grade, in whose class I first had a computer), Mrs. Bachle (sixth grade, who encouraged my love of performance speaking for poetry and narrative), Mrs. Owens (seventh grade, who let me be creative), Mrs. Marsh (who honored me with the eighth-grade English student of the year award), and Mrs. DeKunder (at East Central High School, who made me diagram so many sentences and provided the revise/accept essay format as a clear example of how drafting and editing improves our writing). These women and other educators like Mrs. Gonzalez, Santos, Wagner, and Madame Hurley, showed me how to pursue a love of learning.

I'm so grateful for the people who have been there for a long, long time, being a friend and cheerleader. Tiffany, Jill, Emily, you've told me to go for my dreams of earning a PhD, writing a book, and changing the world. I love you. And to my newer crew, my friends around Waco, Texas, and Baylor University, there are too many to name, but the love and support I have felt from our community is unmatched.

And last, but certainly the most heartfelt and impactful, are thanks to my family. Joe, you are the rock in our family and none of this would be possible without you keeping all of us steady. Eli, you are doing the very best sonning I could ever expect and I can't wait to one day write about that amazing labor you do in our family. Lyla Grace, you are the most wonderful version of a daughter, who makes every effort to stay connected while seeking your own path forward. To my mom and dad, who way oversold how special I am—but still seem to believe it—I cherish your vote of confidence and treasure your love and joy in me. To my sister, you get me. I couldn't ask for more. And to all the other family members who are loving me quietly but proudly, I am so grateful for you.

SELECTED BIBLIOGRAPHY

Alford, A. M. & Miller-Day, M. (Eds.) (2019). *Constructing motherhood and daughterhood across the lifespan.* Peter Lang.

Angelou, M. (2013). *Mom & me & mom.* Random House.

Baxter, L. A. (2011). *Voicing relationships: A dialogic perspective.* Sage.

Brik, R. (2023). *My father's eyes, my mother's rage.* Library and Archives Canada.

Brown, B. (2021). *Atlas of the heart: Mapping meaningful connection and the language of human experience.* Random House.

Buhl, H. M. (2009). My mother: My best friend? Adults' relationships with significant others across the lifespan. *Journal of Adult Development, 16,* 239–249. https://doi.org/10.1007/s10804-009-9070-2.

Callero, P. L. (2009). *The myth of individualism: How social forces shape our lives.* Rowman & Littlefield.

Chodorow, N. (1978). *The reproduction of mothering: Psychoanalysis and the sociology of gender.* University of California Press.

de Beauvoir, S. (1953). *The second sex.* Knopf.

Deakins, A., Lockridge, R., & Sterk, H. (Eds.) (2013). *Mothers and daughters: Complicated connections across cultures.* Rowman & Littlefield.

Fischer, L. R. (1986). *Linked lives: Adult daughters and their mothers.* Harper & Row.

Folbre, N. (2002). *The invisible heart: Economics and family values.* The New Press.

Friday, N. (1977). *My mother/my self.* Random House.

Glenn, E. N., Chang, G., & Forcey, L. R. (1994). *Mothering: Ideology, experience, and agency.* Routledge. https://doi.org/10.4324/97813155 38891.

Gates, M. (2019). *The moment of lift: How empowering women changes the world.* Macmillan.

Gottman, J. (1998). *Raising an emotionally intelligent child: The heart of parenting.* Simon & Schuster.

Hirsch, M. (1989). *Mother/daughter plot: Narrative, psychoanalysis, feminism.* Indiana University Press.

hooks, b. (1984). *Feminist theory: From margin to center.* South End Press.

Jolanki, O. (2015). To work or to care? Working women's decision-making. *Community, Work & Family, 18*(3), 268–283. https://doi.org /10.1080/13668803.2014.997194.

Jung, A.-K., & O'Brien, K. M. (2019). The profound influence of unpaid work on women's lives: An overview and future directions. *Journal of Career Development, 46*(2), 184–200. https://doi. org/10.1177/0894845317734648.

Lorde, A. (2020). *When I dare to be powerful.* Penguin.

McBride, K. (2009). *Will I ever be good enough?: Healing the daughters of narcissistic mothers.* Atria Books.

Miller-Day, M. (2004). *Communication among grandmothers, mothers, and adult daughters: A qualitative study of maternal relationships.* Lawrence Erlbaum Associates. https://doi.org/10.4324/9781410612120.

O'Connor, P. (1990). The adult mother/daughter relationship: A uniquely and universally close relationship? *The Sociological Review, 38*(2), 293–323. https://www.doi.org/10.1111/j.1467-954x.1990.tb00913.x.

Pyke, K. (1999). The micropolitics of care in relationships between aging parents and adult children: Individualism, collectivism, and power. *Journal of Marriage and the Family, 61*(3), 661–672. https:// doi.org/10.2307/353568

Rodsky, E. (2019) *Fair play: A game-changing solution for when you have too much to do (and more life to live).* G.P. Putnam's Sons.

Ruddick, S. (1989) *Maternal thinking: Towards a politics of peace*. Beacon Press.

Russell, A., & Saebel, J. (1997). Mother-son, mother-daughter, father-son, father-daughter: Are they distinct relationships? *Developmental Review, 17*, 1-37. https://doi.org/10.1006/drev.1997.0456.

Seidel, A. J., Majeske, K., & Marshall, M. (2020). Factors associated with support provided by middle-aged children to their parents. *Family Relations, 69*(2), 262–275. https://doi.org/10.1111/fare.12413.

Shrier, D. K., Tompsett, M., & Shrier, L. A. (2004). Adult mother–daughter relationships: A review of the theoretical and research literature. *Journal of the American Academy of Psychoanalysis and Dynamic Psychiatry, 32*, 91-115. https://doi.org/10.1521/jaap.32.1.91.28332.

Thomassen, B. (2016). *Liminality and the modern: Living through the in-between*. Routledge.

van Mens-Verhulst, J., Schreurs, K., & Woertman, L. (1993) *Daughtering and mothering: Female subjectivity reanalysed*. Routledge.

Walters, S. D. (1992). *Lives together, worlds apart: Mothers and daughters in popular culture*. University of California Press.

Walters, M., Carter, B., Papp, P., & Silverstein, O. (1988). *The invisible web*. Guilford Press.

NOTES

Introduction

5 *textbook on mothers and daughters:* Alford, A. M., & Miller-Day, M. (Eds.). (2019). *Constructing motherhood and daughterhood across the lifespan.* Peter Lang. https://doi.org/10.3726/b10841.

5 *I created a podcast:* Our podcast ran for two short seasons and spans just 10 episodes. But it is preserved on Spotify and has great overviews and guests that can get you more acquainted with the topics of adult daughters and daughtering. Alford, A. M., & Miller-Day, M. (2022–2023). *Hello Mother, Hello Daughter* [audio podcast]. https://open.spotify.com/show/2rIS5ykTCTI3M6NvgH6uU1.

5 *woman's personal well-being:* These are a few of the published research articles that show the journey I've been on to explore the topic of daughtering over the past few years: Alford, A. M., & Harrigan, M. M. (2019). Role expectations and role evaluations in daughtering: Constructing the good daughter. *Journal of Family Communication, 19*(4), 348–361. https://doi.org/10.1080/15267431.2019.16433; Alford, A. M. (2021). Doing daughtering: An exploration of adult daughters' constructions of role portrayals in relation to mothers. *Communication Quarterly, 69*(3), 215–237. https://doi.org/10.1080/01 463373.2021.1920442; Alford, A. M. (2024). Daughterwork in times of social upheaval, *Qualitative Research Reports in Communication,* 1–9. https://doi.org/10.1080/17459435.2024.2362212.

6 *other individual person:* Select readings on mother/daughter connections: Bojczyk, K. E., Lehan, T. J., McWey, L. M., Melson, G. F., & Kaufman, D. R. (2011). Mothers' and their adult daughters' perceptions of their relationship. *Journal of Family Issues, 32,* 452–481.

https://doi.org/10.1177/0192513X10384073; Lefkowitz, E. S. (2005). "Things have gotten better": Developmental changes among emerging adults after the transition to university. *Journal of Adolescent Research, 20*(1), 40–63. https://doi.org/10.1177/0743558404271236; Petronio, S. (2002). *Boundaries of privacy: Dialectics of disclosure.* State University of New York Press; Rossi, A. S., & Rossi, P. H. (1990). *Of human bonding: Parent–child relationships across the life course.* Routledge. https://doi.org /10.4324/9781351328920.

6 *fathers in adulthood:* Typically, once daughters are in adulthood they have formed more intense bonds with their mothers than fathers. Bengtson, V. L. (2001). Beyond the nuclear family: The increasing importance of multigenerational bonds (The Burgess Award Lecture). *Journal of Marriage and Family, 63*(1), 1–16. https://doi.org /10.1111/j.1741–3737.2001.00001.x; Birditt, K. S., Miller, L. M., Fingerman, K. L., & Lefkowitz, E. S. (2009). Tensions in the parent and adult child relationship: Links to solidarity and ambivalence. *Psychology and Aging, 24*(2), 287–295. https://doi.org/10.1037/a0015196; Suitor, J. J., & Pillemer, K. (2006). Choosing daughters: Exploring why mothers favor adult daughters over sons. *Sociological Perspectives, 49*(2), 139–161. https://doi.org/10.1525/sop.2006.49.2.139. (Original work published 2006.)

Chapter 1: What Is Daughtering?: The Unseen Role

16 *sense of family:* Nelson, M. K. (2006). Single mothers "do" family. *Journal of Marriage and Family, 68*(4), 81–795. https://doi.org/10.1111 /j.1741–3737.2006.00292.x.

16 *what you've done:* Wilson, J. & Tonner, A. (2020) Doing family: The constructed meanings of family in family farms, *Journal of Rural Studies, 78,* 245–253. https://doi.org/10.1016/j.jrurstud.2020.06.002.

16 *kin work and kinkeeping:* Di Leonardo described *kinkeeping,* or the work of women to maintain familial relationships, as hidden, not because it is conducted in secret but because the work is unacknowledged as social reproductive labor by those who dismiss it or have little understanding of its personal cost. Di Leonardo, M. (1987). The female world of cards and holidays: Women, families, and the work of kinship. *Signs: Journal of Women in Culture and Society, 12*(3), 440–453. https://doi.org/10.1086/494338.

16 *fostering meaningful connections:* Hornstra, M., & Ivanova, K. (2023). Kinkeeping across families: The central role of mothers and stepmothers in the facilitation of adult intergenerational ties. *Sex Roles, 88*(7–8), 367–382. https://doi.org/10.1007/s11199–023–01352–2; Perry-Jenkins, M., & Gerstel, N. (2020). Work and family in the second decade of the 21st century. *Journal of Marriage and Family, 82*(1), 420–453. https://doi.org/10.1111/jomf.12636.

17 *Sociologist Arlie Hochschild described:* Hochschild has written quite
a bit over the years about emotion work and emotional labor, but two
seminal texts are a peer-reviewed article on the topic: Hochschild, A.
(1979). Emotion work, feeling rules, and social structure. *American
Journal of Sociology, 85,* 551–575. And a book: Hochschild, A. (1983).
The managed heart: Commercialization of human feeling. University of
California Press.

17 *Mental, or cognitive labor:* Wayne, J. H., Mills, M. J., Wang, Y. R.,
Matthews, R. A., & Whitman, M. V. (2023). Who's remembering to
buy the eggs? The meaning, measurement, and implications of invisible
family load. *Journal of Business and Psychology, 38,* 1159–1184. https://
doi.org/10.1007/s10869-023-09887-7.

18 *supervisory skill* metaparenting: Robertson, L. G., Anderson, T. L.,
Hall, M. E. L., & Kim, C. L. (2019). Mothers and mental labor:
A phenomenological focus group study of family-related thinking
work. *Psychology of Women Quarterly, 43*(2), 184–200. https://doi.org
/10.1177%2F0361684319825581.

21 *Take what Grier Shields said:* McNeil, L. (2024, August 28). Brooke
Shields and her daughters: How the star raised 2 strong women she's
proud to call her friends (Exclusive). *People.* https://people.com/brooke
-shields-and-her-daughters-how-the-star-raised-2-strong-women
-exclusive-8701638.

27 *idea of multiple mothers:* Hampton, M. R. (1997). Adopted
women give birth: Connection between women and matrilineal
continuity. *Feminism & Psychology, 7,* 83–106. https://doi.
org/10.1177/0959353597071011; Phoenix, A., & Seu, B. (2013).
Negotiating daughterhood and strangerhood: Retrospective
accounts of serial migration. *Feminism & Psychology, 23*(3), 299–316.
https://doi.org/10.1177/0959353512473954; Egan, M., O'Connor,
A. B., & Egan, J. (2022). Creating a new narrative: A theory of how
adopted individuals readjust their adoptive identity in parenthood.
Adoption & Fostering, 46(3), 318–335. https://doi.org
/10.1177/03085759221112449.

29 *try to negotiate:* van Mens-Verhulst, J. (1993). Beyond daughtering
and mothering. In J. van Mens-Verhulst, K. Schreurs, & L. Woertman
(Eds.) *Daughtering and mothering: Female subjectivity reanalysed*
(pp. 160–164). Routledge. https://doi.org/10.4324/9780203359693.
Quote from page 531.

Chapter 2: What Is a Good Daughter?: The Social Landscape

41 *a singular experience:* De Kanter, Ruth. (1993). Becoming a situated
daughter: "Later, when I am big, I will be daddy, so then we will also
have a father in our house"—Hannah, four years old. In J. Mens-
Verhulst, K. Schreurs and L. Woertmann (Eds.), *Daughtering and*

mothering: Female subjectivity reanalysed (pp. 26–34). Routledge.

42 *Organizational researchers define work:* Blustein, D. L., & Duffy, R. D. (2020). Psychology of working theory. In S. D. Brown & R. W. Lent (Eds.) *Career development and counseling: Putting theory and research to work* (3rd ed., pp. 201–236). Wiley.

43 *powerful psychological concept:* Schultheiss, D. E. P. (2009). To mother or matter: Can women do both? *Journal of Career Development, 36*(1), 25–48. https://doi.org/10.1177/0894845309340795.

45 *everyday family life:* Daly, K. (2003). Family theory versus the theories families live by. *Journal of Marriage and Family, 65*(4), 771–784. http://www.jstor.org/stable/3599889.

48 *giving themselves a self-assessment:* Alford, A. M., & Harrigan, M. M. (2019). Role expectations and role evaluations in daughtering: Constructing the good daughter. *Journal of Family Communication, 19*(4), 348–361. https://doi.org/10.1080/15267431.2019.1643352.

50 *of meaningful relationships:* Seligman, M. E. P., & Csikszentmihalyi, M. (2000). Positive psychology: An introduction. *American Psychologist, 55*(1), 5–14. https://doi.org/10.1037/0003–066X.55.1.5.

54 *happy, secure kids:* Winnicott, D. W. (1953). Transitional objects and transitional phenomena. A study of the first not-me possession. *International Journal of Psycho-Analysis, 34 [1953]*, 89–99.

Chapter 3: A Different Kind of Daughter: How Do I Redefine My Adult Daughter Role?

64 *creating shared realities:* Berger, P., & Luckmann, T. (1966). *The social construction of reality: A treatise on the sociology of knowledge.* Anchor Books.

71 *long-term relationship:* Harvey J. H., & Omarzu J. (1997) Minding the close relationship. *Personality and Social Psychology Review,1*(3), 224–240. https://doi.org/10.1207/s15327957pspr0103_3.

72 *support them in this goal:* Taylor, S. E. (2012). Tend and befriend theory. In P. A. M. Van Lange, A. W. Kruglanski, & E. T. Higgins (Eds.), *Handbook of theories of social psychology* (pp. 32–49). Sage Publications Ltd. https://doi.org/10.4135/9781446249215.n3.

74 *experience the same parenting:* Maté, G. (2023). *Scattered minds: The origins and healing of attention deficit disorder.* Avery.

75 *independent from an early age:* Adler, A. (2010). *Understanding human nature* (W. B. Wolfe, Trans.). Martino Fine Books. (Original work published 1927.)

76 *her family relationships:* Some research on birth order has found correlations, but large-scale studies fail to find strong links. Damian, R. I., & Roberts, B. W. (2015). The associations of birth order with personality and intelligence in a representative sample of U.S. high school students. *Journal of Research in Personality, 58*, 96–105. https://

doi.org/10.1016/j.jrp.2015.05.005; Rohrer, J. M., Egloff, B., & Schmukle, S. C. (2015). Examining the effects of birth order on personality. *Proceedings of the National Academy of Sciences, 112*(46) 14224–14229, https://doi.org/10.1073/pnas.1506451112.

76 *Nor has birth order:* Birth order has been shown not to be predictive of personality traits, though it may still be linked to certain behaviors as parents assign roles for their children in the family system: Damian, R. I., & Roberts, B. W. (2015). The associations of birth order with personality and intelligence in a representative sample of U.S. high school students. *Journal of Research in Personality, 58,* 96–105. https://doi.org/10.1016/j.jrp.2015.05.005; Rohrer, J. M., Egloff, B., & Schmukle, S.C. (2015). Examining the effects of birth order on personality. *Proceedings of the National Academy of Sciences U.S.A., 112(*46), 14224–14229, https://doi.org /10.1073/pnas.1506451112.

77 *applied to daughtering:* Bishop, C. L. (2013). Psychosocial stages of development. In Keith, K. D. (Ed.). *The Encyclopedia of Cross-Cultural Psychology.* https://doi.org/10.1002/9781118339893.wbeccp441.

78 *magnetism of togetherness:* Lefkowitz, E. S. (2005). Things have gotten better: Developmental changes among emerging adults after the transition to university. *Journal of Adolescent Research, 20*(1), 40–63. https://doi.org/10.1177/0743558404271236.

81 *enacted both cognitively and behaviorally:* Erikson, E. H., & Erikson, J. M. (1998). *The Life Cycle Completed.* W. W. Norton & Company.

84 *thorns among the roses:* Authors Larsen and McKibban investigated happiness and the quote "happiness is not having what you want but wanting what you have" by Rabbi Hyman Schachtel (1954). They found that happiness is related to both having and wanting. Larsen, J. T., & McKibban, A. R. (2008). Is happiness having what you want, wanting what you have, or both? *Psychological Science, 19*(4), 371–377. https:// doi.org/10.1111/j.1467–9280.2008.02095.x.

87 *Expressive Writing Paradigm:* Pennebaker, J. W. (1997). Writing about emotional experiences as a therapeutic process. *Psychological Science, 8,* 162–166.

Chapter 4: Daughtering Out Loud: Imagining a Society That Sees Us

91 *and higher-level needs:* Blustein, D. L. (2011). A relational theory of working. *Journal of Vocational Behavior, 79*(1), 1–17. https://doi. org/10.1016/j.jvb.2010.10.004.

91 *and community involvement:* Gerstel, N. (2000). The third shift: Gender and care work outside the home. *Qualitative Sociology, 23*(4), 467–483. https://doi.org/10.1023/A:1005530909739.

92 *their contributions recognized:* Schultheiss, D. E. P. (2009). To mother or matter: Can women do both?. *Journal of Career*

Development, 36(1), 25–48. https://doi.org/10.1177%2F089484530
9340795.

94 *in unpaid labor:* Coffey, C., Espinoza Revollo, P., Harvey, R.,
Lawson, M., Parvez Butt, A., Piaget, K., Sarosi, D., & Thekkudan,
J. (2020). *Time to care: Unpaid and underpaid care work and the global
inequality crisis.* Oxfam. https://doi.org/10.21201/2020.5419.

95 *"A rich vocabulary:* Schulz, M. (1975). The semantic derogation of
woman. In B. Thorne & N. Henley (Eds.), *Language and sex* (pp. 64–75).
Newbury House.

95 *while suppressing others:* Ardener, E. (1975). The "problem" revisited.
In S. Ardener (Ed.), *Perceiving women* (pp. 19–27). Malaby Press.

Chapter 5: Intersectional Perspectives on Daughtering

106 *initial sexual revelation:* Bernstein, P. P. (2004). Mothers and
daughters from today's psychoanalytic perspective. *Psychoanalytic
Inquiry, 24*(5), 601–628. https://doi.org/10.1080/07351692409349106.

107 *influence daughters' self-image:* McBride, H. L. (2017). *Mothers,
daughters, and body image: Learning to love ourselves as we are.* Post Hill
Press.

107 *in complex ways:* Crenshaw, K. W. (2017). *On intersectionality:
Essential writings* (p. 255). Faculty Books. https://scholarship.law.
columbia.edu/books/255.

108 *small, everyday instances:* Aptheker, B. (1989). *Tapestries of life:
Women's work, women's consciousness, and the meaning of daily experience.*
University of Massachusetts Press.

109 *site for empowerment:* Brown, E. B. (1989) Mothers of mind. *Sage:
A Scholarly Journal on Black Women 6*, 1 (Summer 1989), 4–11.

110 *daughterly to one another:* Collins, P. H. (2000). *Black feminist
thought: Knowledge, consciousness, and the politics of empowerment* (2nd
ed.). Routledge.

110 *and epistemological worldview:* Evans-Winters, V. E. (2019). *Black
feminism in qualitative inquiry: A mosaic for writing our daughter's body.*
Taylor & Francis Group.

110 *a podcast episode:* Interview with Leah and Mildred Boveda.
Hello Mother, Hello Daughter. "I'm not dismissed." Daughtering as an
analytical framework in the Black feminist tradition. https://open.
spotify.com/episode/6paRGmV6v7t1vvRVjbPMdG.

110 *culture of othermothering:* Evans-Winters, V. E., Pabon, A. J.,
Robinson, T. Y. (2024). *Black women mothering & daughtering during a
dual pandemic: Writing our backs.* Information Age Publishing.

111 *act of survival:* Scholar Andrea O'Reilly analyzed many of the
works by Toni Morrison, then summarized her argument in the text:
O'Reilly, Andrea. *Toni Morrison and motherhood: A politics of the heart.*
State University of New York Press, 2004. One of Morrison's most

popular writings on motherhood is *Beloved*: Morrison, T. (1987). *Beloved*. Alfred A. Knopf.

112 *bits of "female lore"*: Lowinsky, N. R. (1992). *Stories from the motherline: Reclaiming the mother-daughter bond, finding our feminine souls*. Jeremy P. Tarcher, Inc.

112 *systems of oppression*: Woo, M. (2022). Letter to Ma. In *This bridge called my back, fortieth anniversary edition: Writings by radical women of color* (pp. 138–145). State University of New York Press. https://doi.org/10.1515/9781438488295-042.

113 *change the world*: Moraga, C. (2000). *Loving in the war years: Lo que nunca pasó por sus labios* (2nd ed.). South End Press.

114 *died from cancer*: Uzo Aduba shared about her new book during this interview with *People*. Falcone, D. R. (2024, September 24). Uzo Aduba jokes lack of sleep as a mom of an infant is a "crime against humanity": "On another level" (Exclusive). *People*. https://people.com/uzo-aduba-calls-lack-of-sleep-as-mom-a-crime-against-humanity-exclusive-8717008.

Chapter 6: What Do I Owe?: A Daughter's Journey of Responsibility

125 *relational dialectics theory*: Baxter, L. A., & Montgomery, B. M. (1996). *Relating: Dialogues and dialectics*. Guilford.

Chapter 7: Who My Parent Is Now (and Why That Matters)

145 *role reversal oversimplifies the complexities*: Fingerman, K. L. (1996). Sources of tension in the aging mother and adult daughter relationship. *Psychology and Aging, 11*(4), 591–606. https://doi.org/10.1037/0882-7974.11.4.591.

146 *"The cathexis between mother and daughter*: Rich, A. (1976). *Of woman born: Motherhood as experience and institution*. Virago Press.

147 *new and multiple responsibilities*: Marks, S. R. (1977). Multiple roles and role strain: Some notes on human energy, time and commitment. *American Sociological Review, 42*(6), 921–936. https://doi.org/10.2307/2094577.

148 *"a daughter's emotional and psychological growth*: Webster, B. (n.d.). Maternal horizon. In *The Mother Wound psychology glossary*. Bethany Webster. Accessed from https://www.bethanywebster.com/mother-wound-psychology-glossary/.

148 *not even be aware of*: Gawande, A. (2014). *Being mortal: Medicine and what matters in the end*. Metropolitan Books.

149 *as emotion regulation*: Glorioso, C. & Sibille, E. (2011). Between destiny and disease: Genetics and molecular pathways of human central nervous system aging, *Progress in Neurobiology, 93*(2), 165–181, https://doi.org/10.1016/j.pneurobio.2010.11.006.

152 *reaching filial maturity:* Fingerman, K. L. (Ed.). (2001). *Aging mothers and their adult daughters: A study in mixed emotions.* Springer.

152 *they enter motherhood:* Jones, L. (2023) *Matrescence: On pregnancy, childbirth, and motherhood.* Pantheon Books.

154 *in their elderhood:* Dautzenberg, M. G., Diederiks, J. P., Philipsen, H., Stevens, F. C., Tan, F. E., & Vernooij-Dassen, M. J. (2000). The competing demands of paid work and parent care: Middle-aged daughters providing assistance to elderly parents. *Research on Aging, 22*(2), 165–187. https://doi.org/10.1177/0164027500222004.

156 *post on this very topic:* StyrkeSkalVandre (2023, April 15). Has anyone else noticed their parents becoming more socially isolated and volatile as they age? [online forum post]. Reddit. https://www.reddit .com/r/Millennials/comments/1al5ga4/has_anyone_else_noticed_their _parents_becoming_/.

156 *friends and family:* Carstensen, L. L., Isaacowitz, D. M., & Charles, S. T. (1999). Taking time seriously: A theory of socioemotional selectivity. *American Psychologist, 54*(3), 165–181. https://doi.org /10.1037/0003–066X.54.3.165.

158 *unchanged over time:* Kornell, N., & Bjork, R. A. (2009). A stability bias in human memory: Overestimating remembering and underestimating learning. *Journal of Experimental Psychology: General, 138*(4), 449–468. https://doi.org/10.1037/a0017350.

160 *Imagined interactions are cognitions:* Honeycutt, J. M. (2008). Imagined interaction theory. In L. A. Baxter & D. O. Braithewaite (Eds.), *Engaging theories in interpersonal communication: Multiple perspectives* (pp. 77–87). Sage. https://doi.org/10.4135/9781483329529.n6.

Chapter 8: The Difficult Side of Daughtering

166 *These studies have found:* Fingerman, K. L., Huo, M., & Birditt, K. S. (2020). Mothers, fathers, daughters, and sons: Gender differences in adults' intergenerational ties. *Journal of Family Issues, 41*(9), 1597–1625. https://doi.org/10.1177/0192513X19894369.

166 *Sometimes bad feelings occur:* Birditt, K. S., Hartnett, C. S., Fingerman, K. L., Zarit, S. H., & Antonucci, T. C. (2015). Extending the intergenerational stake hypothesis: Evidence of an intra-individual stake and implications for well-being. *Journal of Marriage and Family, 77*(4), 877–888. https://doi.org/10.1111/jomf.12203.

166 *guilt that arises:* Kalmijn, M., de Leeuw, S. G., Hornstra, M., Ivanova, K., van Gaalen, R., & van Houdt, K. (2019). Family complexity into adulthood: The central role of mothers in shaping intergenerational ties. *American Sociological Review, 84*(5), 876–904. https://doi.org/10.1177/0003122419871959.

166 *difficulties could arise for other reasons:* Hanum, L., Newcombe, P., & Scott, T. (2024). A systematic review of intergenerational co-residence between older people and adult children. *Journal of Family Studies, 30(6)*, 968–988. https://doi.org/10.1080/13229400.2024.2363785.

176 *understand this phenomenon:* Weick, K. (1995). *Sensemaking in organizations.* Sage.

179 *A daughter might say:* Tannen, D. (2006). *You're wearing that?: Understanding mothers and daughters in communication.* Ballantine Books.

Chapter 9: The Future of Daughtering

196 *death and dying:* Eldercare responsibilities typically fall to the daughters of the family. Clancy, R. L., Fisher, G. G., Daigle, K. L., Henle, C. A., McCarthy, J, & Fruhauf, C. A. (2020). Eldercare and work among informal caregivers: A multidisciplinary review and recommendations for future research. *Journal of Business and Psychology, 35*, 9–27. https://doi.org/10.1007/s10869–018–9612–3; and Wolff, J. L., Spillman, B. C., Freedman, V. A., & Kasper, J. D. (2016). A national profile of family and unpaid caregivers who assist older adults with health care activities. *JAMA Internal Medicine, 176(3)*, 372–397. https://doi.org/10.1001/jamainternmed.2015.7664.

201 *sense of purpose:* Park, C. L. (2010). Making sense of the meaning literature: An integrative review of meaning making and its effects on adjustment to stressful life events. *Psychological Bulletin, 1(36)*, 257–301. https://doi.org/10.1037/a0018301.

ABOUT THE AUTHOR

Dr. Allison Alford is a communication expert, author, and speaker whose work centers on the everyday experiences of women—especially the things that often go unnoticed. She earned a BA in International Studies with minors in French and Public Relations from Texas A&M University. Together with an MA and PhD in Communication Studies from the University of Texas at Austin, Allison brings both academic rigor and heartfelt curiosity to her research on adult daughters, invisible labor, and the complex relationships that shape women's lives.

Through her writing, teaching, and speaking, she shines a light on "daughtering"—the often invisible role adult daughters play in supporting their families. Her research has been featured in scholarly journals, classrooms, and a podcast. Allison believes in the power of stories to make people feel seen and validated, and she's passionate about helping women reclaim language and frameworks that reflect their lived realities. She loves traveling the world for speaking engagements and collaborations that demonstrate the value and importance of women's experiences in midlife.

Allison is a clinical associate professor at Baylor University and the founder of the firm Good Talk Communication Consulting, where she coaches professionals to speak with clarity, courage, and confidence. When she's not in the classroom or facilitating workshops, she's having real conversations with women in the thick of life, always listening for what needs to be named next.

Allison lives in Texas with her husband, two teenagers, and their pup, Louise.